JOHN SCHREINER'S

BC COASTAL

WINE TOUR GUIDE

whitecap

EDITED BY Carolyn Stewart
COVER DESIGN BY Mauve Pagé and Diane Yee
INTERIOR DESIGN BY Stacey Noyes / LuzForm Design
TYPESET BY Michelle Furbacher
PHOTOGRAPHY BY John Schreiner unless otherwise specified

Printed in Canada by Friesens.

LIBRARY AND ARCHIVES CANADA CATALOGUING IN PUBLICATION

Schreiner, John, 1936–
   John Schreiner's BC coastal wine tour guide : the wineries of the Fraser Valley, Vancouver, Vancouver Island and the Gulf islands.

ISBN 978-1-77050-042-6

   1. Wineries—British Columbia—Guidebooks. 2. Wine and wine making—British Columbia. 3. Viticulture—British Columbia. 4. Vintners—British Columbia. I. Title. II. Title: BC coastal wine tour guide. III. Title: British Columbia coastal wine tour guide.

TP559.C3S334 2011   663'.2009711
   C2011-900849-1

The publisher acknowledges the financial support of the Government of Canada through the Canada Book Fund (CBF) and the Province of British Columbia through the Book Publishing Tax Credit.

11 12 13 14 15   5 4 3 2 1

This is dedicated to the memories of three pioneers of coastal viticulture.

JOHN HARPER, who tested many varieties in his vineyards in the Fraser Valley and later on Vancouver Island; he freely gave cuttings and his sage advice to many coastal vintners.

DENNIS ZANATTA, whose vineyard in the Glenora district south of Duncan supported the grape-growing trials of the Duncan Project and who in 1992 launched Vigneti Zanatta, the first modern-era winery on Vancouver Island.

CLAUDE VIOLET, a beneficiary of John Harper's counsel, who planted the first commercial vineyard in the Fraser Valley at Domaine de Chaberton, the first vineyard-based winery in the Fraser Valley when it opened in 1992.

CONTENTS

WHY I WROTE
THIS BOOK

ALL OF MY WINE BOOKS ARE WRITTEN FOR the same reason: every winery has a wonderful story—and I want to tell it. Winery people, in my experience, are among the most likeable people in the world. Knowing something about them always makes their wines taste better.

Since 2007, I have written three editions of *John Schreiner's Okanagan Wine Tour Guide*, each one larger than the last because of the continual emergence of wineries in the British Columbia interior. I am delighted that many consumers are using that book to enrich their touring experience.

It is obvious that visitors to the coastal wineries should have a companion guide. So should the wineries, many of which have remarkably low profiles. The coastal wineries, being younger than Okanagan wineries, have yet to promote themselves aggressively beyond their local markets. Invariably, consumers are surprised when they learn just how many wineries have opened in the past two decades in the Fraser Valley and on Vancouver Island and the Gulf Islands. *Two wineries in Port Alberni?* Who would have guessed?

With few exceptions, the coastal wineries are small. Many market their wines locally because their production is limited. Excellent Vancouver Island wineries, such as Alderlea Vineyards or Starling Lane to name a few, almost never have their wines in shops and restaurants off the Island. If the wines won't come to you, then this book will guide you to those wines and to what you have been missing.

The coastal wine-touring experience is different from that of the Okanagan. Because the coastal wineries are relatively undiscovered compared with the Okanagan, their tasting rooms, often staffed by winery owners, are not crowded. In fact, some tasting rooms open only on weekends, although most wineries will welcome visitors by appointment. There is much to commend the unhurried touring experience afforded by the coastal wineries.

Coastal wines are distinctively different from those of the Okanagan, reflecting the climate, the soils and the grape varieties. The white wines are typically aromatic and finished crisply because of their bright acidity. The red wines often are medium-bodied with bright fruit flavours. Alcohol levels are almost always moderate, although there can be exceptions when wines are made with tented grapes or in hot years. There are varieties that are exclusive to the coast, or nearly so. These include Madeleine Sylvaner, Madeleine Angevine, Ortega and the Blattner hybrids (Cabernet Foch, Cabernet Libre, Petite Milo and varieties yet to be named). The block of Cayuga at Vigneti Zanatta, where it is turned into a wonderful sparkling wine, is the only Cayuga in British Columbia.

A number of the coastal wineries also buy grapes from the Okanagan to make wines from varieties such as Merlot and Syrah that are unsuitable for the cool and sometimes rainy coastal vineyards. The use of Okanagan grapes is a sensitive issue among the producers. The strict purists make wines only from the grapes suitable to the coast. They believe that region's strength lies in the distinctive flavours of coastal wines. Offering wines from Okanagan grapes blurs this coastal personality. These producers ask why a coastal winery should compete head to head with Merlots from 175 Okanagan wineries when it can make varietals that do not echo the Okanagan. There is much merit in the argument.

That being said, there is nothing wrong with making wines from grapes grown in other regions as long as the label is clear about the appellation from which the grapes come. It is done in wine regions all over the world by producers wanting to offer a broad spectrum of wines to their consumers. In this book, I indicate whether a winery makes wines from coastal grapes only or also from Okanagan grapes. I leave it for you to choose to drink local wines only or wines reflecting other British Columbia terroirs as well. I would hope you try both.

There are more fruit wineries, meaderies and cideries on the coast than in the British Columbia interior. A wine lover with a questing palate and an open mind will find much to admire. These are among the most creative wines fermented anywhere in British Columbia, often with traditions older than grape wines. Mead is one of the oldest fermented beverages in history. The leading mead producers on the coast have revived recipes dating at least from the Vikings.

This guide celebrates not just the distinctive flavours of coast wines. As I have done in other guides, I provide biographies that are a rich mosaic of anecdotes. The colourful owners of the coastal wineries include doctors (three), lawyers, economists, real estate developers, business entrepreneurs, former teachers, a towboat captain and berry farmers, among many backgrounds. I believe that wines are always better when you know the stories behind them.

THE ROOTS OF COASTAL
WINEMAKING

SOME VINTNERS BELIEVE THAT THE SIGNATURE WINE OF Vancouver Island today is made from blackberries. There is symmetry to that contention: the British Columbia wine industry began on Vancouver Island in the 1920s to give the loganberry farmers on the Saanich Peninsula another market for their berries. That berry, full of flavour and high in sugar, was developed by the California judge and gardener, James Harvey Logan, who crossed raspberry and wild blackberry in 1883. It was planted widely on southern Vancouver Island and in the Fraser delta but succumbed to plant diseases in the 1930s. By then, British Columbia wineries—only a handful had opened—had added blueberries and grapes when commercial vineyards were planted in the Okanagan in the late 1920s.

Vancouver Island's first commercial winery, Growers' Wines, opened in 1923 on Victoria's Quadra Street. The first two port-style wines were Logana, made with loganberries, and Vin Supreme, a blend of loganberries and blueberries. A second loganberry winery, Brentwood Products, was established in Saanich in 1927 and changed its name a few years later to Victoria Wineries. S. B. Slinger, the winemaker, also ran his own small winery for several years in Chemainus. The first Victoria Wineries' product to reach the market, sometime in the first quarter of 1930, was Slinger's Loganberry Wine, with a banana-yellow oval label with black and red type. It was available in bottles ranging from 26 ounces (at 50 cents a bottle) and 40 ounces (at 75 cents) through to one gallon in size. The berry supply was so abundant that the winery produced four times as much wine as it could sell. It had 160,000 gallons of inventory by early 1931. By the end of the year, the nearly bankrupt winery was taken over by Growers' Wines, which was managed more successfully by Herbert Anscomb, a contentious figure in the annals of BC wine.

Successful both as a brewery owner and as general manager of Growers' Wines, Anscomb was elected to the provincial legislature in 1933, ultimately becoming the finance minister and the leader of the Conservative party. He brazenly used his position to promote his winery. In 1940, he had a role in blocking T. G. Bright & Co. from opening a plant in British Columbia to bottle its Ontario-made wine. Very few Ontario wines, or even European ones, were listed by the government liquor sales monopoly; the first California wines were listed only in 1962. In this protected market, the handful of British Columbia wineries thrived. Growers' was eventually sold to the Rothmans, a South African cigarette manufacturer, and changed its name to Jordan & Ste-Michelle Cellars. The Victoria winery closed in 1977, moving to a new winery in Surrey. That closed after Brights took over Jordan and moved production to a new winery near Oliver in 1981.

There was no commercial winemaking on Vancouver Island from 1977 until 1992, when Vigneti Zanatta opened. However, there was a continuing interest in grape growing, supported by the federal government's determined research to identify vines suitable for both the Island and the Fraser Valley. The Dominion Experimental Farm at Agassiz included grapes among its research soon after it was established in 1888. The annual report published by the Farm in 1937 reported the following:

"In the early history of this Farm there were extensive plantings of grapes and over one hundred varieties were tested. Plants on the whole proved hardy and were vigorous but most kinds were too late to mature satisfactory crops in the majority of years . . . During the past three decades many new varieties have come on the market, many of which are early maturing kinds and which have not been adequately tested. There is a very considerable interest in grape growing at the present time in

TENTED VINEYARD IN THE SPRING

FRASER VALLEY FARM

this section of the province, both for table stock and wine manufacture."[1]

Beginning in 1937, the Farm renewed its trials with such varieties as Patricia, Campbell's Early, Mary, Lindley, Portland and Fredonia, which for the most part are labrusca hybrids. Ultimately, at least 25 varieties were tested. The vines even survived inundation during the 1948 Fraser River flood. "In fact, of all crops grapes appeared best able to stand flood conditions," according to the 1948 report by the Farm's superintendent. "This was true throughout the Fraser Valley. One vineyard in Hatzic was under 10 to 15 feet of water and yet recovered fully."[2] A few years later that vineyard was pulled out and another was planted on high ground. The Farm continued to test grapes into the 1960s before coastal viticulture research was handed off to the research station in Saanichton. A test vineyard was established when a quarantine station was set up there by Canada Department of Agriculture's plant protection division.

There was renewed interest in coastal grape growing after the hard, vine-killing winters in the Okanagan in 1964–65 and again in 1968–69. In the latter winter, temperatures plunged to −37°C (−35°F) and the grape harvest in 1969 was reduced by two-thirds from the year before. "Since then commercial wine companies have become more interested

1 Excerpts from papers in the personal files of John Vielvoye.
2 Vielvoye papers.

in the growing of wine varieties on coastal B.C.," wrote Harry Andison, the director of the Saanichton station, in a paper published by Canada Agriculture in 1971.[3] "The three commercial wineries in the coastal areas of B.C., Andrés Wines, Port Moody, Growers' Wine Co., Victoria, and Villa Wines, New Westminster, are particularly interested in Aurora, Foch, Himrod, Seibel 9549, Seyval, Schuller, New York Muscat and Vineland 37034 . . . As a result of our tests, these wineries are now planting the above varieties in nurseries and in trial plantings in the coastal areas of B.C." He wrote that one of the wineries (believed to be Growers') had planted "a large acreage" at Duncan. These trials produced no significant results, likely because Villa closed and both Growers' and Andrés shifted focus to the Okanagan and to grape varieties better suited for table wines than these hybrids. When John Vielvoye, the Ministry of Agriculture's grape specialist in Kelowna, launched new grape trials near Duncan in 1981, he could find no trace of the Growers' planting.

That vineyard, however, had stirred interest. In 1981, John Grayson— who has since been involved in both fruit wine production and distilling on Hornby Island—considered growing four hectares (10 acres) of grapes on his hobby farm near Duncan. Responding that October to a letter from Grayson, John Vielvoye replied: "The grapes at Duncan that you refer to, were planted on the Indian Reserve by the Indian people. Aid was provided in terms of advice and some plants via the Growers' Wine Co. (now Ste-Michelle) and Mr. Andison, director of the Agriculture Canada Research Station at the time. The planting was much smaller than you stated; it was closer to six acres. It was not maintained, nor were records of it kept."[4]

Nothing if not determined, Grayson replied in December that his research suggested "good ground to support the idea of a west coast commercial grape growing possibility [and] the need for a test planting in the Cowichan Valley." He added a list of 14 grape varieties, saying he wanted to source 300 vines of each. Grayson is believed to have consulted with John Harper, then a viticulturist in the Fraser Valley, who advised that the soil on his farm was too fertile for a vineyard.

---

3   Vielvoye papers.
4   Correspondence in author's files.

DENNIS ZANATTA
AND THE DUNCAN PROJECT

BY THIS TIME, JOHN VIELVOYE WAS GETTING NUMEROUS requests about establishing vineyards on Vancouver Island and in the Fraser Valley. In 1981, he joined an investigation of Cowichan Valley sites by members of the British Columbia Land Commission. "At one point, we ended up at [Dennis] Zanatta's property and the question came up about the suitability of that area for growing grapes," Vielvoye recalled in an interview with me.[5] "Dennis had some plants around a swimming pool at the house. He was quite interested in finding out himself whether it was suitable or not, and so he offered to make his property available for a test site." That was the beginning of what is known as the Duncan Project. Thirty-one varieties of grapes were planted in 1983—vinifera such as Ortega, Chardonnay and Auxerrois; hybrids such as Castel and Okanagan Riesling; and numbered hybrids from the Summerland research station's breeding program. After considerable frost damage during the cold 1985–86 winter, 17 varieties were removed, among them Chardonnay, Pinot Blanc and even Vidal. Some 22 additional varieties were planted in 1987 while more were pulled out in 1989. The ministry decided to stop supporting the grape trials. By then, however, Dennis Zanatta had plunged ahead independently, and his decision to grow grapes for a winery soon inspired others.

Dennis Zanatta emigrated from Treviso in northern Italy in 1950 as Dionisio, changing his name to the more accessible Dennis at the suggestion of a Vancouver relative. He worked in Vancouver as a tile setter and was so good that he was offered a similar job in Hawaii. Instead, he moved to Vancouver Island in 1958, buying a large farm in the Glenora district, just south of Duncan. He operated a dairy farm for about 10 years before starting his own tile business and, in 1992, establishing a marble quarry in the Cowichan Valley. "Dennis made his own wine and used to import grapes, like most Italians did," Vielvoye says. It was

---

5   Interview with John Vielvoye, July 3, 2010.

natural to plant a few vines as well. Vielvoye recalls that he had Léon Millot around the swimming pool and grew table grapes nearby.

The Duncan Project was done on a shoestring. Dennis not only provided the land, he cultivated what was required for vines and provided posts, trellis wires and some of the labour and equipment. "He had a pond across the road from where we established the vineyard that was used as an irrigation source," Vielvoye remembers. "The Ministry of Agriculture put in an irrigation system, using that particular pond. Later on, we put in a weather station and the bird netting and used that as a demonstration project in order to demonstrate the benefits of irrigation for the grape crop and small fruits. And the bird netting demonstrated the benefits of having netting for bird protection rather than noise makers." Much of the routine vineyard work was also done by Vielvoye and other ministry staff, including summer students. The project ended prematurely after the ministry stopped funding the work in the vineyard. "In the last couple of years, it basically fell back on Dennis," Vielvoye says.

At harvest, the grapes were processed with a press and a destemmer that Dennis had imported from Italy. The juice, saved into 20-litre glass carboys, was shipped to the federal research station at Summerland where Gary Strachan, one of the staff scientists, made the wine. The finished samples came back to be assessed in annual tastings, often arranged in a hotel in Cowichan Bay. "We had quite a cross-section of politicians and local people for wine tastings," Vielvoye remembers. These included some of Dennis Zanatta's winemaking friends. One of those friends, on tasting a wine made from Cayuga, suggested the grape would be excellent for sparkling wine. When Dennis took full control of the vineyard, he kept Cayuga. He also planted more Auxerrois, Ortega and Pinot Gris, along with three clones of Pinot Noir (a variety not in the Duncan Project trials).

Eventually, Dennis extended the vineyard to a full 30 acres. That was the combined total owned by several family members and was the largest vineyard on Vancouver Island. Since Dennis's death in 2008, ownership has been consolidated by his daughter Loretta, whom he sent to wine school in Italy in the late 1980s, and his son-in-law Jim Moody.

Vigneti Zanatta, the first new commercial winery on Vancouver Island in 65 years, opened in 1992.

"The Duncan Project was not long enough or funded at a level which would permit the assessment of wines produced from mature vines," Vielvoye lamented in a 1992 report on the project.[6] "However, based on the results of this project, continued evaluation of new potentially suitable varieties for coastal areas appears justified. The best of varieties grown in parts of other countries with cool climate conditions . . . are similar to those varieties in the Duncan Project that appear to have promise."

JOHN HARPER:
THE MAN WHO WAS INFATUATED WITH VINES

JOHN HARPER IS A LEGEND IN BRITISH COLUMBIA grape growing, having contributed significantly to viticulture in the Okanagan, the Fraser Valley and finally on Vancouver Island. Toward the end of his long career—he died in 2001 in his 85th year—John almost succeeded in creating an estate winery on the Island. While that ambition was frustrated by his partners, he was generous in help-

VERNA AND JOHN HARPER (PHOTO COURTESY OF BETTY TOPOROWSKI)

ing others. Port Alberni's Vaughan Chase, the owner of Chase & Warren Estate Winery, turned to John for vines when he first started planting. In 1974, for a small vineyard in suburban Vancouver, Giordano Venturi sourced vines from Ayl Moselle, as John called his vineyard and nursery. "That was the beginning of a long, if not intimate, relationship," Giordano says. In 1987 he and Marilyn Schulze visited Vancouver Island

---

6   The Duncan Project: Summary Report, British Columbia Minister of Agriculture, Fisheries and Food, 1992, 22 pages.

for the first time to look for vineyard property. They were advised to inspect a new vineyard in the Cowichan Valley. "Here we met John again in the middle of the couple of acres that he had just planted," Giordano recalls. "It was because of his reassuring presence on the Island that we moved to our present location a few months later." Some years later, the Venturi Schulze Estate Winery released a tribute wine from vines they had purchased from John, calling it Harper's Row.

Harper was born in Calgary in 1915 and grew up there, where one of his teachers was William Aberhart, the future Social Credit premier who was then teaching mathematics. Harper's interest in growing plants came from his father, a former New Brunswick orchard operator. "I was involved in horticulture by the time I was eight years old," Harper said in a 1993 interview. "I was exhibiting vegetables in fairs."[7] His interest in wine developed when he began working for Canadian Pacific, both in hotels and on railroad dining cars. He joined the army when war broke out and ended up in doing military catering in England, North Africa and Italy. "The last four years of the war, I was looking after catering for a very large Canadian hospital," he said. He dealt with wine buyers from Christie's in London and further educated his palate. "You classified everything against the best of Bordeaux," he remembered. "A lot of people in Canada did not like the particular style of wines that I liked when I came back because they weren't as sweet as the people in Canada liked them."

He was unable to resume his career in the food industry after the war because he had contracted amoebic dysentery and malaria. "He came back from the war very ill," says Betty Toporowski, a Harper daughter born after the war. "He would spend lots of winters in the hospital."[8] As he got his strength back, he went to work in construction and for a number of years was a superintendent with a Vancouver builder of banks, schools and other commercial structures.

After returning from Europe, John and Verna, his wife, settled first on two hectares (five acres) near Steveston and began a plant nursery. When the 1948 Fraser River flood inundated the property, they resumed nursery operations in Delta. When urban development overtook that site,

---

7   Interview with author.
8   Interview with author.

they sold it (at an advantageous price) and, in1970, bought property in Cloverdale, on what is now a residential area on 180th Street. "He was basically semi-retired and he started growing all the grape plants and doing things with the Ministry of Agriculture," his daughter recalls. His experimental vineyard has been variously reported as being between one and two hectares (two and five acres) in size and with as many as one hundred varieties. (In fact, Betty Toporowski believes that her father may have tested as many as one thousand varieties.)

"Because he had a southwest-facing property, it was pretty much ideal for growing the varieties he had there," says Ron Taylor, who was a winemaker at Andrés Wines from 1970 to 1992. Harper's friendship with Harry Andison, the director at the plant quarantine station at Sidney on Vancouver Island, seems to have given him access to many vines for his trials. "I had known him because I had been head of the Richmond Berry Growers Association, as president, and he was an entomologist," Harper said. "I had known him before he became director of the station and we became good friends. We always used to have a bottle of wine at lunch. He paid his turn and I paid my turn."

Established in 1965, the quarantine station began importing vines from nurseries in England. "That was the place we could get them at that time because amateur winemaking in England was already well under way," Harper explained. "These varieties that were allowed [included] Müller-Thurgau and Ortega. We had about nine or ten from Germany. And we had four or five French hybrids, such as Seyval Blanc, Maréchal Foch and Léon Millot, the Alsatian red." Some of the German varieties came through Dr. Helmut Becker, the renowned director of viticulture at Germany's Geisenheim institute. Becker contributed most of the varieties grown in the Okanagan for trials—the so-called Becker Project—that ran from 1977 through 1985. Becker and Harper, kindred spirits when it came to enthusiastic wine drinking, travelled together on several occasions. And Harper taught himself enough German to read technical literature and books on German viticulture.

Over time, Harper emerged as one of British Columbia's most knowledgeable consultants on grape growing. Whether he made a living as a consultant is another matter. John Vielvoye, who began working as the provincial government's grape specialist in 1966, says: "John loved to talk, so he would provide free advice to anybody that would ask for it. Most of the wineries that were on Vancouver Island at the time would come to him. John would spend time with all these people. In the meantime, Verna [his wife] did all the work." John Bremmer, who was a manager at Andrés at the time, has a similar recollection of his meetings with Harper: "Verna would be working out in the greenhouse and then she would be working out in the field. Meanwhile, John and I would be talking about all sorts of things. And then she would scurry in and make us lunch. The woman was just a dynamo."

By the early 1980s, Harper's neighbourhood in Cloverdale was being taken over by urban development and, as a result of rezoning, his property taxes jumped sharply. That led to a search for property on Vancouver Island for the trial varieties he was growing. A decade earlier a Duncan letter carrier named Wilson had purchased vines from Harper. When he began making wine he brought samples to Cloverdale for comparative tastings, since Harper also made his own wine. The promise of Wilson's wines drew the Harpers to the Cowichan Valley in the mid-1980s and to the property now owned by Blue Grouse Estate Winery.

In 1984, a company called Bitec Development Corp., which was listed on the Vancouver Stock Exchange and was run by John Harper Jr., announced plans to raise $1.5 million for an estate winery. The elder John Harper, described as having 14 years' experience in viticulture, was named an "Associate" of the project. "It was through Mr. Harper's knowledge, expertise and research that our winery project was conceived," the company said in a press release.[9] When it did not go ahead, a company called Westwood Vineyards emerged, building a laboratory in which to create vine stock through tissue culturing, funded with money raised under the federally sponsored Scientific Research Tax Credit program. Unfortunately, it all unravelled when Revenue Canada began auditing how funds had been spent. The project was put into bankruptcy. The elder John Harper had nothing to do with how the funds had been spent because he was busy in his vineyard.

---

9   Copy in author's files.

On Christmas Eve in 1990, John and Verna Harper started over again on a new property nearby. Here, they planted close to one hundred different varieties in a postage-stamp vineyard and built a greenhouse to continue their horticultural work with flowers and other plants. "If the two of us have our health, we'll go for a farm winery," he told the *Vancouver Sun* in 1992. "But that's questionable because of our age, don't you know." Even though his friend, the postman Wilson, came to help drive the tractor, time eventually ran out. They sold the property in 1998 to John Kelly, who launched Glenterra Vineyards two years later. Kelly planted additional acreage but continues to make two blended wines from the 40 experimental varieties remaining in the Harper test block. He is one of the many who benefitted from John Harper's infatuation with the vine.

CLAUDE VIOLET
PIONEERS FRASER VALLEY WINE GROWING

DEVLIN MCINTYRE, NOW THE OWNER OF SALT SPRING Vineyards, was a surgeon in Abbotsford and a hobby grape grower in the mid-1980s, when he and another hobbyist founded the Fraser Valley Wine Growers Association. They were flattered when Claude Violet came to their meetings. Here was a man with a long French heritage in wine growing, who owned, with his wife Ingeborg, the first and largest commercial vineyard in the Fraser

CLAUDE VIOLET

Valley. His presence brought credibility, along with technical support and encouragement, to wine growing in coastal British Columbia. There were no wineries with their own vineyards in the coastal regions when Claude and Inge emigrated here from Europe in 1981. At the time of his death in 2008, several dozen wineries had opened.

Claude was born in Paris in 1935. Although he trained as a banker in Germany, he could claim nine generations of wine growing. "My family originated from a small village in the south of France called Corsavy, which is located between Perpignan and the border of Spain in Roussillon," Claude wrote in a short memoir in 1995. "Beginning in 1644 Manaut Violet grew grapes. Six generations followed his example in Corsavy, gradually increasing the size of their farm. In 1856 Simon Violet moved his area of operation to Thuir, a large town of 3,000 inhabitants, and in 1866 founded the firm producing the aperitif Byrrh. Under the guidance of my father, Jacques Violet, the eighth generation of the family in the business, the company expanded to the point where it was producing 100,000 bottles a day in 1935. He enlarged the volume of the Thuir cellar by building the largest wood vats in the world, one of which, having the capacity of 1,000,000 litres, [is] still the record today."[10]

In the 1950s, the Byrrh firm amalgamated with two other aperitif producers (the makers of Dubonnet and Cinzano). When that was swallowed by the even larger Pernod Ricard firm, the Violet family sold its interest. Claude, after apprenticing as a banker, returned to the wine business, operating a 200-hectare vineyard in the south of France and a wine brokerage company in Spain, both from a base in Switzerland. By the late 1970s, with Cold War tensions high, Claude and Inge decided to move their family away from Europe.

"During 1979 . . . Ingeborg and I travelled extensively in the USA looking for a suitable site for a vineyard," Claude wrote. "We considered many locations in New York, Connecticut, Virginia, Texas, New Mexico, California, Oregon and Washington. Preferring to live in Canada, we also visited Ontario and the Okanagan. We decided on the Fraser Valley, which we felt had the best possibilities for our needs, specializing in white wines." In interviews later, Claude elaborated on the details not included in that spare outline. He joked that the United States was not a fit because he knew nothing about baseball. He judged the Niagara Peninsula too cold for successful viticulture. The Okanagan had a more favourable climate but it was too far from the big Vancouver market (it

---

10 *Personal History and Experiences of Mr. Claude Violet*; copy in author's files.

would be 20 years before Vancouver wine tourists began showing up in the Okanagan in significant numbers). Claude reasoned he would most likely succeed if his vineyard and winery was close to Vancouver. His reasoning influenced several other wineries, most notably Township 7, to open in the Fraser Valley.

In 1980 Claude sold his business in Switzerland and initiated a search for a Fraser Valley vineyard. "With the help of Mr. John Harper, who has excellent knowledge of the Fraser Valley," he wrote, "we found after a month of research, a 55 acre farm with a southern exposure on 216th Street in Langley." Satisfied with the temperature, rainfall and soil data provided to him by the provincial government, Claude bought the farm and moved his family from Europe in 1981.

Even with its southern exposure, the property needed more work. The slope was contoured to eliminate low spots, drainage was installed so that the vines would not grow with wet feet, and the soil chemistry was balanced. Some 14 hectares (35 acres) were planted with vines imported, for the most part, from Germany and France. The major varieties chosen were Bacchus, Madeleine Angevine, Madeleine Sylvaner, Ortega and Chardonnay.

To this day, Bacchus, an aromatic white, is one of Domaine de Chaberton's flagship varieties (and is also grown by a few Vancouver Island vintners). This is a cool-climate variety developed by a German research station and classified officially in 1972. Claude, knowing that the vine performed well in German conditions similar to those of the Fraser Valley, ordered his vines from a Mosel nursery. As well, Bacchus was among the vines included in the Becker Project in the Okanagan and proved a success in Kelowna-area vineyards. "I chose that variety because I saw it growing well in the Mosel," Claude told me.[11]

Madeleine Angevine and Madeleine Sylvaner were varieties developed in the 1850s in the Loire, another cool-climate wine region. While Claude was aware of this history, he started his 1983 plantings with vine cuttings from Mount Baker Vineyards in Washington State, a winery not far south of Sumas in the Fraser Valley. "It must grow here as well,"

---

11 Schreiner, John. *Chardonnay and Friends*. Orca Book Publishers, 1998, page 24.

Claude reasoned.[12] Subsequently, these varieties have been planted on Vancouver Island and by wineries in the Shuswap, another tribute to Claude's influence. Domaine de Chaberton opened in 1991, the first estate winery in the Fraser Valley and the cornerstone to much of the winery development since.

VALENTIN BLATTNER
AND HIS DISCIPLES

IN 2000, A CHANCE MEETING WITH SWISS PLANT breeder Valentin Blattner turned Salt Spring Island winemaker Paul Troop into a strong proponent of Blattner's hybrid grapes. Wines from these varieties, which have appeared only in recent vintages, show the promise to give coastal wines even greater individuality than they have already.

Valentin, who was born in 1958, acquired an interest in grapes as a youth, when his parents sent him to learn French in Switzerland's French-speaking wine-growing region. Subsequently, he worked with an agricultural chemical company in Mozambique. The experience turned him against dousing chemicals on plants. When he returned to Switzerland and to viticulture, he decided to devote himself to developing varieties of grape vines that, because of their natural resistance to disease, would not require the application of chemical sprays. In the early 1990s, he planted a small vineyard in

ABOVE: VALENTIN BLATTNER IN THE VINEYARD. (PHOTO COURTESY OF PAUL TROOP) BELOW: PAUL TROOP

12 Ibid, page 89.

Soyhières, in the canton of Jura in northwestern Switzerland (not a traditional wine region) and set about to develop thousands of new hybrid varieties. One of his earliest varieties is Roselle, a 1986 cross of Bacchus and Seyval Blanc, which he produces only at his small winery. "I make 3,000 bottles for the whole world," he told a Vancouver Island conference in 2005. "You have to see me to get it."

Several of his successful crosses employed Cabernet Sauvignon as one of the parent varieties. Valentin believed that the tannin in that variety provides a good defence against disease and thus was a character that should be imported to the new varieties. The variety also has both red and white genes, enabling the development of both red and white grape varieties from this parent. The varieties on the other side of many crosses are Maréchal Foch and Léon Millot, red hybrids that were developed by Alsace plant breeder Eugene Kuhlmann (1858–1932). Valentin contends that Kuhlmann's disease-resistant reds "saved the vineyards" of France in the 1920s and 1930s when various fungal diseases were ravaging vinifera plantings.

In 1998, Euro Nursery and Vineyards in Harrow, Ontario, began a trial of Blattner hybrids, with 2,800 Blattner varieties primarily grown from seeds. The nursery also began trials for a few years at a satellite planting at the Centre for Plant Health, a federal government research station near Sidney on the Saanich Peninsula. Valentin visited these projects in 2000 and booked a side trip to Salt Spring Island. There, he stayed at the bed and breakfast operated by Jan and Bill Harkley, who were just planting vines for what became Salt Spring Vineyards when it opened in 2003. The Harkleys and Paul Troop, who was helping them, were so taken with Valentin that they went to Switzerland that fall to help pick grapes and learn from the Blattner vineyard.

Born in Victoria in 1955, Paul had spent more than two decades in a variety of technical jobs with the telephone company and, on the side, was a passionate home winemaker. As Paul puts it, he "pulled the pin" on the phone company and came to Salt Spring Island in 1996. Here, he found a job managing a vineyard near Ganges owned by Bruce Smith, a Victoria developer who briefly considered developing a winery. One day, he was instructing Paul how to spray the Pinot Noir, Chardonnay

HORNBY ISLAND VINEYARD (PHOTO BY PATRICIA JONES)

and Pinot Gris, adding that the sprayer could be turned off at the row of Maréchal Foch because that variety did not need spraying. "I thought to myself, why not plant the whole vineyard in Foch and skip the sprayer," Paul says.

A year later, he discovered that Valentin Blattner had a similar view. In 2002, when Paul started his own vineyard not far from Salt Spring Vineyards, he not only planted Maréchal Foch, he got cuttings of several Blattner varieties from a Saanich grower and, in the fall of 2002, he went to Harrow and selected almost 60 other Blattner varieties. These vines, planted in 2003 and 2004 in Paul's vineyard, have served primarily as the mother block for most of the Blattner plantings on Vancouver Island, the Gulf Islands and the Fraser Valley. The Blattner proselytizer in the Fraser Valley has been David Avery of Lotusland Vineyards. He and Paul briefly were partners in grape propagation and vineyard development but now operate independently.

Alderlea Vineyards at Duncan was the first winery in British Columbia to release a Blattner varietal commercially, a barrel-aged red wine from the 2005 vintage that was made mostly from a grape called Cabernet Foch. Roger Dosman, the co-proprietor at Alderlea, released the wine under a proprietary name, Fusion. In 2010, he changed the name to Matrix after selling the trademark to a large Argentine winery that was

FORT BERENS VINEYARD

GARRY OAKS VINEYARD

selling a Fuzion brand in Canada. The second commercial release, one hundred cases from the 2009 vintage, was a white blend released by Salt Spring Vineyards. Because the wine was ready before the winery had settled on a name, it was released merely as "Blattner White."

It is probable that many Blattner varietals will end up under proprietary labels, if only because the grapes just have the plant breeder's number. However, a handful of the Blattner varieties have been named. Cabernet Foch and Cabernet Libre are red varieties; Epicure and Petite Milo are whites. The procedure for christening these varieties can be quite informal. Petite Milo, a vine that has small bunches, was named for a small-statured Vancouver Island vineyard manager named Milo. If the Blattner varieties find a commercial following, they will differentiate the coastal wineries from those in the Okanagan or the Similkameen. "Every region has to have a variety which is the signature of that region," Valentin told Vancouver Island grape growers in 2005.[13]

"This whole process is still evolutionary," says Roger Dosman, who continues to trial new Blattner varieties. "We are introducing a new wine to the region. It probably won't be successful until you get two or three producers who are doing a respectable job of making the wine. And maybe even [under] one common name."

---

13 Author's notes.

VANCOUVER ISLAND SOUTH

ALDERLEA VINEYARDS

In the early 1990s, when he was new to growing vines, Roger Dosman sought advice from the veteran viticulturist John Harper. "He is probably the reason for my success," Roger told an industry seminar 15 years later. "I learned a lot from him. I learned to view the world from the eye of the grapevine and what it needs."

Roger has probably looked through the eyes of more grapevines than anyone on Vancouver Island by continuously sorting the winners from the losers. He started his vineyard in 1994 with three hectares (7 acres) and about 30 varieties, and he has probably worked with twice that many because he never hesitates to replace those that don't measure up. "Things like Ehrenfelser and Rotberger and Würzer and all the other goofy stuff that you try," he says. "We have expanded the vines that have done very well for us." Today, Maréchal Foch commands one-fifth of the vineyard, followed by Pinot Noir and Pinot Gris. And the trials continue. He has planted several of the Blattner hybrids. Since 2005 he has been making a successful red wine from one Blattner variety—but he pulled out another when he found it got the same diseases as the variety it replaced.

Roger is realistic. "Our region is a very marginal wine region," he told that seminar. "That's a fact of life." That is why it is critical to identify the appropriate varieties and not squander precious vineyard sites on the "goofy" varieties.

Growing grapes and making wine is a long way from Roger's previous career. Born in Vancouver in 1948, he got a degree in urban geography. But rather than becoming a town planner, he went to work in his father's autobody shop in 1972 and bought the business four years later. After deciding to switch careers in 1988, he reflected, "I used to make money fixing cars. Now I make a living. There is a big difference."

He and Nancy, his wife, spent four years investigating vineyard property, looking in the Similkameen Valley, the Fraser Valley and the Sunshine Coast before buying this farm in the Cowichan Valley in 1992. The property, with a sunbathed south-facing slope, is only 10 minutes from Duncan (which originally was called Alderlea). The location on a dead-end road gives the Dosmans the privacy Roger prefers, which is why the tasting room now is open by appointment only. "If you are going to be open, you have to be open all the time," he says. "It is just not in the cards for me anymore." The winery makes between 1,600 and 2,000 cases a year. Roger sells it all directly to customers, restaurants and wine stores on the Island and keeps weekends free for his family. He is as disciplined personally as he is with his vineyard, where the vines grow like soldiers on parade.

Getting it right in the vineyard is fundamental because Roger buys no grapes. "My commitment is to use only estate-grown fruit," he says. "It always has been that and always will be. Quite frankly, I think I make some very

OPENED 1998

1751 Stamps Road
Duncan, BC V9L 5W2

T   250.746.7122

W www.alderlea.com

WHEN TO VISIT
By appointment

ROGER DOSMAN

CONTINUED NEXT PAGE...

ALDERLEA VINEYARDS

CONTINUED

distinct wines. When you taste our Pinot Noir over the years, you know it's Alderlea Pinot Noir."

For all his realism, he does have some sentimental attachments among his varieties, most notably Viognier, a late-ripening white. To succeed on Vancouver Island, it is tented in spring (in other words, accelerated under a temporary plastic cover for several weeks) and ideally has a dry, hot climate for the rest of the year.[14] The grapes can ripen to produce 15 percent alcohol wines. Roger's first Viognier vintage in 1998, a year so warm that the grapes ripened without tenting, yielded 16 cases of exceptional wine. "We had a bidding war for the wine," he recalls. He had been considering pulling out the Viognier until the first release became a cult wine. "I think you have to create a bit of excitement for your winery," he said later.

Alderlea's most recent outstanding Viognier vintage was 2009, another warm, dry season. "It is a killer," Roger said prior to releasing the wine. "It is the best white wine we have ever had."

---

14 Tenting is comparable to starting tomato plants in a greenhouse. Since vines cannot be moved into a greenhouse each spring, the greenhouse conditions are created by stretching a white fabric tent over the plants in spring, for two weeks to two months. The heat that is trapped under the tents accelerates the development of grape clusters. The objective is to get the grapes ripe before the mid-October rains. In 1998, Venturi Schulze Vineyards was the first winery on Vancouver Island to tent some of its vines in spring. The technique is effective but, because it is labour intensive and costly, only a few wineries practise tenting.

All of Alderlea's wines are well crafted. The whites include Bacchus, Pinot Gris, Gewürztraminer, Angelique (a white blend) and, of course, Viognier. Reds include a regular and a reserve Pinot Noir, a wine called Matrix (formerly Fusion) from the Cabernet Foch (a Blattner red), and Clarinet, the winery's very fine, barrel-aged Maréchal Foch. Hearth, a port-style wine, is also excellent.

AVERILL CREEK VINEYARD

As Andy Johnston tells it, the First Nations word for this valley, Cowichan, means a warm place. That was one reason that he planted 30,000 vines on Mount Prevost's slope after deciding against establishing his winery in either France or New Zealand. He argues, provocatively, that much of the Okanagan is too hot for producing the delicate and finessed Pinot Noir wines that are his obsession.

A medical doctor who was born on a Welsh farm in 1947, Andy practised medicine in Alberta for about 30 years as the founder of a chain of 24 walk-in clinics. In the 1990s he decided that "there are only so many patient visits in me" and so he started his education as a wine-maker by working the 1998 vintage at Villa Delia in Tuscany. A contact there opened the door to work the 1999 vintage at McGuigan Wines in Australia. That led to a vintage opportunity in the south of France in 2000 and then to a pair of New Zealand wineries, notably the Pinot Noir specialist, Escarpment Vineyard in Martinborough.

In between these assignments, Andy bought and planted this south-facing Cowichan Valley slope. The modernistic winery, in which the first vintage was made in 2004, offers a panoramic view over the valley, both from its tasting room and from the Tuscany-inspired flagstone courtyard. The setting is so beautiful that the winery also serves as a wedding venue.

Andy devotes most of his time to meticulous management of the 12-hectare (30-acre) vineyard, tenting some vines in spring and then covering it totally with bird netting when colour appears in the red grapes. He has employed a succession of winemakers trained, cru-cially, in the cool-climate viticulture of New Zealand. Daniel Dragert, the winemaker who took over the cellar in 2008, is a Vancouver Island native with a winemaking degree from Lincoln University in Christchurch. After graduating, Daniel came back to Canada in 2007

ANDY JOHNSTON

and spent a year at Red Rooster in the Okanagan before joining Averill Creek.

Averill Creek has quickly become one of the largest wineries on Vancouver Island, producing about 5,000 cases a year. The volume enables Andy to sell his wines in Vancouver and as far afield as Alberta. The quality allows Averill Creek to break down the Lower Mainland's perceived disinterest in Island wines.

OPENED 2006

6552 North Road
Duncan, BC V9L 6K9

T 250.709.9986

W www.averillcreek.ca

WHEN TO VISIT
Open daily 11 am – 5 pm mid-April through October, weekends in winter; and by appointment

MY PICKS

The Gewürztraminer is delicate and spicy, with a dry finish. The Pinot Grigio is light and crisp, standing deliberately in contrast to the rich, barrel-fermented Pinot Gris. Somenos Rosé is a refreshing wine for summer. The Pinot Noir is a classic, tasting of cherries and with a velvety texture. Prevost is Andy's big red, a blend of Maréchal Foch, Merlot and Cabernet Foch. Foch-éh is a playful, Beaujolais-style red and Cowichan Black is an excellent fortified blackberry wine.

BLUE GROUSE ESTATE WINERY

By the time this book is published, Hans Kiltz, the most educated scientist among British Columbia vintners, may have sold this winery and retired, having made nearly 20 excellent vintages. Whatever transition occurs here, his style of winemaking—flawlessly correct—has given Blue Grouse a strong following among both its consumers and peers. Giordano Venturi, one of the owners of Venturi Schulze Vineyards, was so impressed with one Blue Grouse Pinot Gris that he rose from his table to send a highly complementary email to Hans. At the time, Giordano was working on a thesis on Pinot Gris. He believed that the Blue Grouse wine was one of the finest he had ever had.

On the Blue Grouse website, Hans tells of making wine as a hobby after moving in 1989, with wife Evangeline and their family, to this Cowichan Valley property, which included a small vineyard. One of John Harper's experimental vineyards, which had suffered some neglect, the property was quickly whipped into shape. Hans drew on his veterinary background and also tapped the advice of winemaking relatives in Germany to create this winery.

"My scientific degrees helped me to do this," Hans says. "It is not much different, winemaking and veterinarian medicine. Both are half science and half art. When you do operations, you have to imagine things because the animal doesn't talk to tell you where the pain is. It's a sort of art, you know."

Born in Berlin in 1938, Hans has four scientific degrees: one in veterinary medicine, one in tropical veterinary medicine, one in fish pathology and one, a doctorate, in microbiology. As an employee of the United Nations' Food and Agricultural Organization, he worked in both Asia and Africa, once managing a laboratory with 42 employees. Drawn repeatedly to Africa, where he first began working in 1965,

Hans returned reluctantly to Germany about two decades later, when his two children had reached high-school age. That lasted about a year.

"If you are used to life in Africa, you cannot easily get back to a European lifestyle," Hans says, explaining how a much-travelled man with his credentials ended up growing grapes on Vancouver Island. "The other problem, of course, is when you are 50, you won't get a job anymore. You are on your own." So in 1988, intending to apply one of his degrees to fish farming, he came to Vancouver Island. As it happened, British Columbia's aquaculture industry went into a slump. Hans had to turn his hobby winemaking into a business.

The 12.5-hectare (31-acre) Blue Grouse property has an excellent southwestern exposure. The varieties grown include Ortega, Pinot Gris, Siegerrebe, Bacchus and Müller-Thurgau. The primary red is Pinot Noir, nurtured to produce a rich and expressive wine without tenting. Blue Grouse makes wines only from its own grapes. "We were one of the first ones trying to establish an identity for Vancouver Island wine," he

OPENED 1993

4365 Blue Grouse Road
Duncan, BC V9L 6M3

T 250.743.3834

W www.bluegrousevineyards.com

WHEN TO VISIT
Open 11 am – 5 pm Wednesday
to Sunday, April through
September; 11 am – 5 pm
Wednesday to Saturday, October
through December; 11 am –
5 pm Saturday, January through
March

HANS KILTZ

CONTINUED NEXT PAGE...

BLUE GROUSE ESTATE WINERY

CONTINUED

says. He is among those firmly opposed to making wine on the Island from Okanagan grapes.

Blue Grouse's reputation is built on its whites and on Pinot Noir. The winery also has an exclusive wine called Black Muscat—exclusive because Hans never gave cuttings to any other grower. The variety was propagated from a few vines, perhaps of Hungarian origin, that were in the vineyard when Hans bought the property. "I gave the grapes to a home winemaker, a friend of mine, and he made a wonderful wine from it," Hans recalls. Soon, Hans was making about 800 litres (175 gallons) annually of an aromatic dry red, aged in American oak barrels, a wine unique in British Columbia.

MY PICKS

I agree with Giordano Venturi about the fine Pinot Gris here. But also try the Ortega, Siegerrebe, Gamay Rosé and the Pinot Noir. You will have to buy the Black Muscat without trying it first, as it is usually unavailable for tasting, but it is worth the venture.

CHERRY POINT ESTATE WINES

Economist Xavier Bonilla, the third and current owner of Cherry Point, served three presidents of his native Colombia between 1982 and 1994. On the side, he managed his own dairy farm there, where employees milked about 50 cows daily. Throughout that career, Xavier also nursed a passion for wine.

"When I had the dairy farm, I was always dreaming of wine," he says. "I also took many trips to Europe, checking out wineries in Rioja, Duero and Ebro [in Spain]. There are areas [in Colombia] that I was scouting out, desert areas that could have a fantastic potential and nobody has thought about it. I have been doing research on wine for 15 years." He finally realized that dream late in 2009, when he was able to purchase Cherry Point from the Cowichan Indian Band.

A pioneer of Cowichan Valley grape growing, Cherry Point was opened in 1994 by Wayne and Helena Ulrich. There is a coincidental parallel between Wayne's career and Xavier's. Born in 1947 in Colombia, Xavier took a master's degree in agriculture from the University of Wisconsin before going

OPENED 1994

840 Cherry Point Road, RR3
Cobble Hill, BC V0R 1L3

T 250.743.1272

W www.cherrypointvineyards.com

WHEN TO VISIT
Open daily 10 am – 5 pm

RESTAURANT
Bistro for brunch and lunch May through September daily except Monday

XAVIER AND MARIA BONILLA

CONTINUED NEXT PAGE...

CHERRY POINT ESTATE WINES

to work for the government. Wayne formerly was an Agriculture Canada lending officer, whose clients attracted him to the vineyard lifestyle.

Wayne and Helena retired in 2004. Xavier inquired about buying the winery but the Cowichan Indian Band got there first, inspired by the success the Osoyoos Indian Band was enjoying with Nk'Mip Cellars in the Okanagan. Nk'Mip is a joint venture with Vincor, the largest producer and marketer of wine in Canada. Lacking a similar alliance, the Cowichan had less success in penetrating markets.

Xavier brings the energy of an entrepreneur to running Cherry Point. He and his wife, Maria, a professional translator, moved to Vancouver in 1990, when their son and daughter were pursuing advanced degrees at the University of British Columbia. Using the capital from selling his Colombia farm, Xavier first started a lawn maintenance business in West Vancouver. When that successful business was sold a few years later, he became a coffee roaster—and sold that successful business several years later. Then he and Maria opened a fine restaurant, selling it shortly before buying Cherry Point. The restaurant experience stands them in good stead in managing Cherry Point's popular bistro.

Xavier has made a fresh start with a new winemaker, Dean Canadzich. Born in Western Australia in 1966, Dean was drawn to wine by working in vineyards after getting a diploma in horticulture. Deciding there was more opportunity to make wine in Canada than in the overcrowded Australian industry, he moved to the Okanagan's La Frenz Winery in 2007. Becoming Cherry Point's winemaker was especially attractive because Katherine, his wife, is a Vancouver Island native.

Xavier and Dean have refreshed portions of Cherry Point's 8.5 hectares (21 acres) of vineyard, replacing underperforming varieties with Epicure and Cabernet Libre, both promising Blattner hybrids that Dean believes will give him more blending options. When he took over the

DEAN KANADZICH

cellar after the 2009 harvest, he imposed his mark on the wines with clever blending. The Ortega's fruity aromas and flavours were improved by adding 20 percent Siegerrebe to the blend. Bête Noir, formerly made just with Agria, is a mellower red after being blended with Castel.

Xavier is committed to making only estate-grown wines. Perhaps the exception will be fortified blackberry wine, made primarily with wild berries. Cherry Point was the first Island winery to release this fruit wine. Xavier remembers being impressed with the wine when, on his first visit to Cherry Point a decade ago, he was given a bottle. The winery provides a ready market for the local pickers, who bring thousands of pounds of berries here every summer.

MY PICKS

The Ortega/Siegerrebe blend shows appealing fruitiness. The Gewürztraminer has delicately spicy flavours, while the Pinot Gris has crisp citrus flavours. Bête Noir, equal parts Agria and Castel, is a dark, full-bodied red. My choice of the blackberry wines is Solera, a barrel-aged wine incorporating five or more vintages to achieve a fine, port-like richness.

CHURCH & STATE WINES

In 2009, most of the tanks and related winery equipment were shipped from this winery to the South Okanagan, where Church & State has leased a processing facility and built a new winery just off Black Sage Road. While there may be less to see in the cellar at Brentwood Bay, the key attraction—the expansive tasting room and the restaurant with vineyard views—remains open. And the wine shop offers Pinot Gris and Pinot Noir from the 3.6-hectare (nine-acre) Island vineyard, as well as all of the award-winning wines that winemakers Jeff Del Nin and Bill Dyer make in the Okanagan.

The Brentwood Bay winery's other attraction is a location on the road to Butchart Gardens, long the premier tourist attraction on the Saanich Peninsula. That figured in the business plan in 2000, when the promoters of what was then called Victoria Estate Winery were raising money. Their offering circular described it as "a winery accessible to the highest tourist bus traffic in British Columbia." That is why they built what a real estate agent later called a "trophy property," which opened in 2002.

Within two years, the winery was failing, likely because the wines were too mediocre to convert the passing tourists into repeat customers. When Kim Pullen took over the winery late in 2004, he sent nine wines to the VQA tasting panel and all failed. He decided to dump 16,500 cases of wine and relaunch as Church & State. A former tax lawyer, he had experience turning around a business, having taken over a failing fish farm in the 1990s. By the time he sold the company to Norwegian interests, it had annual sales of $25 million. Kim has started several other businesses as well and is still the owner of a large marina in Sidney, not far from the Brentwood Bay winery. "I knew that, over time, I could make this into something," he recalls his thinking as he took over Victoria Estate. "Great building, great location."

KIM PULLEN

He had no wine background other than a consumer's interest. "Mainly I just drink wine," he said. "I didn't drink beer, didn't drink a lot of spirits." He was born in Victoria, into a military family, and had a peripatetic upbringing as his father moved "from army camp to army camp" in Canada and Europe.

To start Church & State with a clean slate, he hired a storied consulting winemaker, Bill Dyer of California. Bill had started consulting after 20 years as winemaker for Sterling Vineyards in the Napa Valley. His first client in British Columbia was Burrowing Owl Estate Winery, where he made the wine from 1997 through 2003. His distinctive full-bodied wines won a cult following for Burrowing Owl. In 2005, Bill joined Church & State after a two-year absence from British Columbia. He was impressed that Kim was buying and planting vineyards a short distance from Burrowing Owl's Black Sage Bench vineyard. Subsequently, Australian-trained winemaker Jeff Del Nin also moved from Burrowing Owl to Church & State.

While most Church & State wines are grown and produced in the South

OPENED 2002
(AS VICTORIA ESTATE WINERY)

1445 Benvenuto Avenue
Brentwood Bay, BC V8M 1J9

T 250.652.2671

W www.churchandstate
wines.com

WHEN TO VISIT
Open 11 am – 6 pm daily May to October; Friday through Sunday in winter

RESTAURANT
Open 11:30 am – 3:30 pm Wednesday to Sunday; closed in winter

CONTINUED NEXT PAGE...

CHURCH & STATE WINES

CONTINUED

Okanagan (where the winery owns or controls 49 hectares (121 acres) of first class vineyard land), Brentwood Bay's vines are capable of producing fine Pinot Gris and Pinot Noir table wines. Kim and his winemakers have also made sparkling wine from these grapes.

In early 2008, Kim came close to selling the Brentwood Bay winery to a would-be winery owner from Alberta, until the financing fell through. The winery is now managed as a showcase for all Church & State wines. The word is getting around to the bus tours, and others, that it is worth stopping to taste the bold, ripe wines that win double gold medals in leading competitions.

MY PICKS

Everything, but especially the Chardonnay, the Pinot Gris, the Merlot, the Cabernet Sauvignon, the Meritage, the Syrah and Quintessential, the winery's premium red.

COBBLE HILL VINEYARD

Tim and Colleen Turyk's decision to start a winery had several tributaries. For a number of years, they have had a summer home at Shawnigan Lake. They had become so involved with the community that their son, Christopher, worked several summers at Amusé Bistro, the town's upscale restaurant, while pursuing studies at the Culinary Institute of America in Napa and later as a sommelier. His passion for food and wine, particularly wine, rubbed off on his parents. As well, their social and golfing circles in Vancouver include William Knudsen, a lawyer and a partner in SpierHead winery in Kelowna. That fired Tim's interest in investing in a winery just as he began to wind down, somewhat, from a business career in the fishing industry.

OPENING PROPOSED FOR 2011

2915 Cameron-Taggart Road
Cobble Hill, BC V0R 1L0

WHEN TO VISIT
To be established

Born in Victoria in 1951, he got into fishing through a summer job in a Prince Rupert packing house while he was completing an economics degree at the University of British Columbia. In 1972, Tim bought a boat and spent the next four years as a commercial fisherman. His partner was Colleen, whose father was in the fishing business as well. In 1978, with his father-in-law, he founded Bella Coola Fisheries, based in Delta, which is believed to be the fourth-largest fish packer on the coast. While Tim is not planning to leave the business in the near future, he talks of lightening the load there to spend more time on Vancouver Island. After a few months of winery ownership, late in 2010, he realized that he is probably exchanging one load for another. CONTINUED NEXT PAGE...

COBBLE HILL VINEYARD

CONTINUED

Cobble Hill Vineyard anchors a 13-hectare (32-acre) farm not far from Shawnigan Lake and within sight of the Merridale Estate Cidery. The nearby location of the cidery, one of the top-rated food and beverage destinations in the Cowichan Valley, contributed to Tim's decision to buy the farm in 2010 after three months of research. The previous owner, Bill Mattison, had planted about a hectare of Maréchal Foch vines in 2006 and begun building a winery when he changed his mind and sold the property. Tim saw it as the opportunity for a quick start in the wine business, beginning with the 2010 vintage. With help first from Averill Creek's Andy Johnston and then from the winemaking team Sara and Daniel Cosman, Cobble Hill Vineyard made about 200 cases of red wine.

The 100-year-old heritage farmhouse here has been turned into a winemaker's residence. The original winery has been expanded to include more tanks and a barrel cellar as well as an attractive tasting room. Tim sees the tasting room as a focal point for visitors, the place where he expects to sell half the winery's production as it grows to 2,000 to 3,000 cases a year. For the next several years at least, Tim will be buying grapes from other Cowichan Valley vineyards. He does intend to plant at least two more hectares of vines. Since he is consulting on this with Daniel Cosman, a propagator of Blattner vines, it is a safe bet that some Blattner varieties will soon be grown here.

"There is probably room for another 15 acres [six hectares of vines] but I don't know if that is really in the cards," says Tim. "I don't want to make it a burdensome thing. I don't want to get out of the fish business. But I am perfectly willing to take [the winery] to the next step, as long as I have good people to do it with me."

DAMALI WINERY & VINEGARY

With this vineyard and lavender farm, Dave and Marsha Stanley and their business partner, Alison Philp, believe they have brought a bit of Provence to the Cowichan Valley. Even the new farmhouse and bed and breakfast, built in 2007, was designed by Victoria architect Pamela Charlesworth in a south of France style. They are not the first to note the valley's Provence personality. James Barber, the author and chef who lived on a Cowichan Valley farm until his death in 2007, famously described it as the Provence of the North.

Both Alison, a former manager of the Duncan Chamber of Commerce, and the Stanleys grew up in this charmed valley. Dave was born in Duncan in 1954 and met Marsha when she was still in high school. Alison, Marsha's best friend, was the maid of honour when Dave and Marsha married, and then godparent to their children. While Alison has lived in the Cowichan Valley all her life, a lack of local jobs sent Dave and Marsha to northern Alberta in 1978. He worked with an oilfield service company while she began the studies that led to her profession as a chartered accountant

OPENED 2010

3500 Telegraph Road
Cobble Hill, BC V0R 1L4

T 250.743.4100
   1.877.743.5170 (toll free)

W www.damali.ca

WHEN TO VISIT
To be established

ACCOMMODATION
Two bed-and-breakfast units

MARSHA STANLEY, ALISON PHILP (CENTRE) AND DAVE STANLEY (PHOTO BY ENISE OLDING)

CONTINUED NEXT PAGE...

DAMALI WINERY & VINEGARY

CONTINUED

and business valuator. They moved to Vancouver in 1985, where Dave earned a diploma in petroleum technology and then took up a career in the engineering department at BC Gas (now FortisBC).

"I always sort of missed the Island," Dave admits. When he was able to retire early in 2005, he and Marsha decided to return to their Cowichan Valley roots. They had conceived of farming lavender the previous summer, while visiting lavender farms near Port Townsend on Washington's Olympic Peninsula. "If it grows here," Dave told himself as they looked across to Vancouver Island, "it'll grow there."

Soon, they were driving around the Cowichan Valley to look for a farm, with Alison invited along for her local knowledge. By the time they found the rundown sheep farm on busy Telegraph Road, Alison had agreed to become their business partner and move into the old farmhouse. It was a bit of a homecoming for both women, who had grown up not far from here and ridden by the farm many times. The three sealed the partnership by calling the business Damali, a Mediterranean-sounding word crafted from the first letters of their given names.

"One of the things we had discussed as we were thinking about buying property was to combine a vineyard and lavender, very much like Provence," Dave says. In 2006, they put in a trial plot of 600 lavender plants, a hectare (2.4 acres) of grapes, 30 fig trees and seven olive trees. They also kept the sheep, the poultry, the fruit trees and some native trees on the 5.2-hectare (13-acre) farm. Since then, the lavender plot has grown to 12,000 plants. They have developed a growing range of lavender products, including soaps, bath salts, hand lotions, face creams, culinary lavender, flower bundles and massage oils, among others.

Dave, a wine lover and long-time home winemaker, branched first into wine vinegar with 2009 vintage Ortega wine purchased from another winery. "We will not make vinegar out of just any wine," he

ALISON AND MARSHA AMONG LAVENDER
PLANTS (PHOTO BY ENISE OLDING)

says. "Great vinegar comes from good wine. You can't make nice vinegar from bad wine." In the spring of 2010, Damali began selling two Ortega wine vinegars, one of them infused with lavender.

The winery was licensed just before the 2010 vintage. Dave made Pinot Gris with purchased grapes, Castel for a red sparkling wine and Damali's most unusual wine, a lavender Gewürztraminer. "We had been asked by many people if we make a lavender wine," Dave says. The technique is straightforward: he makes lavender tea sweetened to the same sugar level that the grapes have naturally at harvest. The two are blended in equal proportions and then fermented like a white wine, producing an aromatic dry wine (Dave prefers dry wines).

Damali may supplement its own wine production with a red or two purchased from another winery (with due credit on the back label), as it will take a few years to mature the farm's own red. However, there will be no grapes or wine here from the Okanagan. "I want to stay island," Dave says. "Why not support what is in your backyard?"

MY PICKS

Current range not tasted.

DE VINE VINEYARDS

Whatever the reason for starting a winery, romance comes into it sooner or later. In John and Catherine Windsor's case, they planted vines on their Saanich property to enhance the romance of the landscape. Eventually, they found themselves in the wine business.

John was born in 1947 in Steyning, a picturesque village in Sussex, England, with a colourful history (it is believed that Alfred the Great's father, Ethelwulf of Wessex, was originally buried in the local church). In 1970, after becoming an associate (and later a fellow) of the Royal Institute of Chartered Surveyors, John set out to see the world and came to Vancouver. A year later Catherine, who was born in Hawaii and was working for a leading restaurant chain there, came to Vancouver on vacation and met John within a week. They soon teamed up as a couple, launching a successful company to manage and invest in real estate.

Their company, North American Land, once managed assets in Canada and several major American cities, subsequently specializing in a portfolio of medical buildings in Atlanta. Their daughter, Kirsten, manages that business because John considered himself retired after selling the Canadian side of the business in 1995 and becoming deeply involved for nine years as a director and chair of Covenant House, a Vancouver charity working with youth.

Several years ago they bought a 10.4-hectare (23-acre) property in central Saanich, building a home there and converting a spacious barn into a glass-blowing studio for Chris Windsor, one of their sons. The property is on a ridge with a great view. They decided to improve on it with a vineyard. The four blocks, called Matthew, Mark, Luke and John, were planted in 2007 and 2008 with Pinot Gris, Pinot Noir and Grüner Veltliner. They planned to sell the organic grapes to Winchester Cellars on the other side of Old West Saanich Road until that winery closed in 2009. So the Windsors recruited one of its former owners, Ken

JOHN WINDSOR (PHOTO BY ANNA BULLOCK, BK STUDIOS)

Winchester, as their winemaker. They bought the equipment of the Gabriola Island Winery, which had just gone into receivership, and tested the equipment by making small quantities of Pinot Gris, Pinot Blanc and Pinot Noir in the 2009 vintage.

The winery, now their passion, will remain comparatively small, producing no more than 2,000 cases a year. "Our pro forma," says John, speaking like the businessman he is, "tells us that if we do about 2,000 cases a year, we will cover our operating costs. It won't provide any return on the capital to Cath and I, but we are not driven for that."

"This has all grown over time," Catherine says and laughs. "It started with 'let's have a piece of property so our son can blow glass' [and grew to] 'let's plant a few grapes so we have some nice landscape' to, 'oh, my goodness, we own a winery.' Whatever we do, we will do well. Neither one of us like to do anything that is less than the very, very best."

OPENED 2010

6181B Old West Saanich Road
Saanichton, BC V8M 1W8

T 250.665.6983

W www.devinevineyards.ca

WHEN TO VISIT
Open noon – 5 pm Saturday and
Sunday, May through September

KEN WINCHESTER (PHOTO BY ANNA BULLOCK, BK STUDIOS)

MY PICKS

Pinot Gris

DEOL FAMILY ESTATE WINERY

The Deol family is the classic hard-working immigrant family. Surgit Deol, the scion of the family, was born in 1930, and he can still set the pace for pruning in the winery's 7.2-hectare (18-acre) vineyard. Before bringing his family to Canada from the Punjab in 1980, he ran a family farm. The crops included grain, corn, cotton, sugar cane and rice, supplemented by livestock. The Deols collected the property taxes in their village and remitted them to the government. On the side, Surgit taught school.

"We always worked hard," says Gary, his son, who was born in 1961. "If you don't work, life is not good." It is a philosophy he shares with his older brother, Gurdip, who was born in 1956. They added to their workloads in 2008 by turning a red dairy barn on their farm north of Duncan into a winery, utilizing the grapes from the vineyard they have planted since 2000. As industrious as they are, the family was surprised by the challenges of running a winery. In 2010, they had the winery up for sale. "Too much work," Gary says.

When the family immigrated, they came first to Duncan and made a hard-scrabble living, doing such things as picking salal berries and harvesting holly. In 1982 they moved to Oliver and bought a small orchard and also laboured in vineyards, including Covert Farms and the Shannon Pacific Vineyard on Black Sage Road. Gary spent more than a decade working with Lanny Martiniuk, the South Okanagan's foremost propagator of grapes who now, with his family, owns Stoneboat Vineyards.

When the fierce Okanagan sun caused some health concerns for the family, the Deols moved back to the Cowichan Valley in 1999. Now experienced grape growers, they planted vines the following year, on what had formerly been a dairy farm. Beginning in 2004, the early vintages were sold to other wineries until this winery was developed. "It is hard to grow grapes here," Gary says, reflecting on the challenge

GARY DEOL

of the Island's periodic cool seasons. "It is not as easy as it is in the Okanagan."

The vineyard is planted primarily with Gamay and Maréchal Foch, with small plots of Pinot Gris and Pinot Noir along with a little bit of Chardonnay, Orange Muscat and early-ripening Schönburger. Gary is considering adding Siegerrebe, in part to produce sweeter wines from that aromatic variety. The winery's first vintage, in 2007, was made by a consulting winemaker who subsequently opened a grape propagation business. To help make subsequent vintages, Gary engaged Jim Moody, the co-owner and winemaker at Vigneti Zanatta.

OPENED 2008

6645 Somenos Road
Duncan, BC V9L 5Z3
T 250.746.3967
W www.deolestatewinery.com

WHEN TO VISIT
Open 11 am – 4:30 pm Monday
to Saturday, mid-May through
mid-October

PICNIC AREA

The winery is well located, just south of the busy highway to Lake Cowichan. The landscape here is that of a working farm, still dominated by the former dairy barn. The winery, however, is in a new building, complete with a barrel cellar. The winery's tasting room, with a commanding view of the vineyard, is located separately, in a century-old farmhouse that has been attractively restored. The ambiance is friendly, with no pretentions, reflecting the personalities of the owners.

MY PICKS

The Pinot Gris is crisp and the Pinot Noir is light and charming. Fans of bigger reds will go for the Gamay and the Somenos Red, a blend that includes Maréchal Foch.

DIVINO ESTATE WINERY

Famously hard-headed, Divino founder Joe Busnardo once told a newspaper reporter that "I don't buckle to nobody . . . I starve first." He showed his grit in 1996, when he moved the winery from the Okanagan, after selling the 32-hectare (70-acre) vineyard there, relocating to a Cowichan Valley property half the size.

As part of the move, he shipped 11,000 cases of finished wine and almost 6,000 cases of bulk wine from the Okanagan winery. He planned to sell it from his Cowichan wine shop, continuing Divino's business without interruption while the new Vancouver Island vineyard was developing. When the Liquor Licensing and Control Branch found out, they suspended Joe's licence. Outraged, he pleaded his case before the Liquor Appeal Board, scoring a crucial victory that allowed him to keep his licence and continue selling the wine. To this day, you will still find bottles of Okanagan wines for sale among the Cowichan wines at Divino.

Joe, born in 1935 in Treviso, is a descendent of generations of Italian winemakers. An agriculture school graduate, he came to Canada in 1954, working as a labourer. In 1967, because he had "never liked any plants but grapes," he bought raw land south of Oliver, on the west side of the Okanagan Valley. All other vineyards then grew hybrid grapes. Joe insisted on planting vinifera. He was ahead of his time: wineries refused to pay a premium for what were surely superior grapes. For a few years, he worked as a tractor operator and let the birds eat the grapes. Finally in 1982, he built his own winery.

Cuttings from that Okanagan vineyard, including Trebbiano, Chardonnay, Pinot Grigio and Pinot Noir, were used to establish the Cowichan Valley vineyard. Joe relocated partly to "slow down" and partly because he and Barbara, his wife, wanted a change from the Okanagan's torrid heat.

After a decade and a half of slowing down on Vancouver Island, Joe actually considers retiring. One would not guess it, however, when tasting wines with him. He is infectiously enthusiastic about wine as he holds court two afternoons a week in the compact tasting room.

Growing grapes on Vancouver Island has its own challenges, Joe has found. With characteristic irreverence, he has noted some on his wine labels. There is a raccoon on the Gamay Cabernet because raccoons seem to favour those varieties; and there is a squirrel on the Chardonnay because squirrels favour that grape. The Merlot Cabernet's deer graze the vineyard all season long, when they find a way though the fence. However, the salmon on the Pinot Gris merely signals a great food and wine pairing.

MY PICKS

Current range not tasted.

OPENED 1982
(IN THE OKANAGAN)

1500 Freeman Road
Cobble Hill, BC V0R 1L3

T 250.743.2311

W www.divinowine.ca

WHEN TO VISIT
Open 1 pm – 5 pm Friday and
Saturday and by appointment

JOE BUSNARDO

DOMAINE ROCHETTE WINERY

Domaine Rochette, which released its first able wines late in 2010, was licensed in 2006 so that it could ferment its own grapes legally for wine jelly. The winery's marketing arm, Epicure Selections, produced several jellies, including a Blush, a Blanc de Blancs and a Pinot Noir. "These did very well and are still doing very well," says Epicure founder Sylvie Rochette. "But we can sell just so many." So the wines surplus to the jelly program are being bottled for the retail wine market. The wine is, after all, just one more product line from Epicure, Canada's largest direct seller of food products. The company has grown from four spice mix products in 1991 to more than 190 products.

Sylvie, born in Clermont, Quebec, was at Laval University, planning to get a law degree, when a strike closed down teaching in 1976. She came to Victoria to visit a friend and just stayed on the west coast. Interested in food and cooking, she developed such delicious spice blends for her own kitchen that friends encouraged her to turn the hobby into a business. She set up Victorian Epicure to distribute the products, initially at farm markets and trade shows on Vancouver Island and then through grocers and other food retailers. But as the business began to thrive, she found the enormous amount of travelling was eating into time for her family and other interests.

She resolved that with a radical change of business plan. In 1996, she set up Epicure Selections, the company's catalogue division, and began selling the products directly to consumers through house parties. That was the business model that worked well for Tupperware and it has worked just as well for Sylvie. The company now has a network of thousands of salespeople across Canada, selling cookware and food products, including the wine jellies, through house parties and the catalogue. For regulatory reasons, the table wines cannot be sold through this network.

The business was based in Victoria until 2003, when Epicure bought a 32-hectare (80-acre) parcel of agricultural land on the Saanich Peninsula as a location for a larger production and distribution centre. The land itself was not in great shape because previous owners had been selling the topsoil. Sylvie set out to rejuvenate its productivity with hay crops and a vineyard. Subsequently, she has planted about 5,000 hardwood trees, including 3,500 walnut trees. Such dedication to recovering the land's agricultural values is entirely in keeping with Sylvie's social philosophy. Epicure supports a number of charities and maintains a foundation that is involved in food security issues across Canada. And since 2004, Sylvie, who has a second home near Côtes du Rhône in France, has taken time to volunteer in Madagascar (where she also buys vanilla beans) with Dentists Without Borders.

Epicure's vineyard began with 3,000 Pinot Noir vines in 2003. Now 2.8 hectares (seven acres) in size, it also includes Maréchal Foch, Ortega and Schönburger. John Brickett, the vineyard manager, is gradually replacing the white varieties with Swiss-developed Blattner grape varieties, thought to be more disease resistant. Petite Milo and Epicure, two Blattner crosses that were christened in Vancouver Island vineyards, are promising white wine varieties. There are a number of other test plots of Blattner vines under evaluation in the Epicure vineyard.

Since the first harvest of Pinot Noir in 2006, the wines have been made by Paul Troop, also the winemaker at Salt Spring Vineyards. As the vineyard came into production, it did not take long for the volume of wine to exceed the needs of the wine

OPENED 2006

10555 West Saanich Road
North Saanich, BC V8L 6A8
T 250.656.5751
W www.epicureselections.com

WHEN TO VISIT
No tasting room

CONTINUED NEXT PAGE...

DOMAINE ROCHETTE WINERY

CONTINUED

jelly program. The first releases include modest volumes of wines from 2007, 2008 and 2009—Pinot Noir, Ortega and Maréchal Foch.

Domaine Rochette is not currently planning to open a tasting room. The wines are released through private wine stores and to restaurants on southern Vancouver Island. But one can only speculate about the prospects of this winery should Sylvie turn her marketing attention to this side of her business.

MY PICKS

Current range not tasted.

DRAGONFLY HILL VINEYARD

Narrow, winding and bordered by forest, Old West Saanich Road still retains the ambiance of what it once was: a stagecoach route on the Saanich Peninsula. One of the roadhouses at which passengers refreshed themselves was here, where Carol Wallace first planted vines in 1993, after acquiring this bucolic farm. Her stepfather, a former Ontario grape grower, suggested she plant vines.

"A lot of people had berry farms," Carol recalls. "I wanted to grow something that was not prickly and that did not make me crawl on my knees to pick." After reading a government report on Cowichan Valley grape trials that was published in 1992, she decided to plant Ortega, Auxerrois and Schönburger. But she was not entirely sure how to proceed because of the conflicting advice she found in reference books. So she telephoned Cowichan Valley grape grower Dennis Zanatta, on whose farm the grape trials were conducted.

"I said, 'I don't know what to do,'" she admits. "He said, 'Do it the way you would like to see it, the way that makes

OPENED 2008

6130 Old West Saanich Road
Victoria, BC V9E 2G8

T 250.652.3782

W www.dragonflyhillvineyard.com

WHEN TO VISIT
By appointment

CAROL WALLACE

CONTINUED NEXT PAGE...

DRAGONFLY HILL VINEYARD

you happy, so you are happy in the vineyard. Don't worry about the books.'" So she laid out the vineyard adopting organic practices, though the use of treated wooden vineyard posts has denied her organic certification. The vineyard, originally less than a hectare (two acres) in size, has rows three metres (10 feet) apart, perhaps the widest spacing on the Island. "You base everything on the tractor," Carol explains. Her elderly John Deere needs that much clearance between the rows, especially when transporting the big sprayer. However, this also gives the vines plenty of sunlight and good air movement, resolving some challenges of Island viticulture.

Born in 1959, Carol grew up in a Niagara Falls neighbourhood populated with Italian home vintners. Her father, a Scot, was drawn into the hobby, and he soon had his daughter involved. "My job was to start the siphon," she remembers. After she moved west, she developed a career in the public service, including spending many years as a clerk of the citizenship court.

Carol did not set out to open a winery. The Victoria Estate Winery, which began development in 2000, promised to buy fruit from Carol and other new growers on the Saanich Peninsula. When it came time to do business, the price offered for the grapes was unacceptably low. Carol sold her grapes to other Island wineries. Salt Spring Vineyards, one of the buyers, made vineyard-designated wines from her grapes. "That's when I realized I was doing a pretty good job as a grape grower," she says.

When Paul Troop, the winemaker at Salt Spring Vineyards, agreed to make her wine, Carol created Dragonfly Hill, opening in 2008 in a converted tractor barn. The winery's name is inspired by the dragonflies in the nearby ponds. The insects are featured on the winery's labels, which, Carol says, were designed for her by a Victoria tattoo artist. The script on the labels is Carol's own penmanship. "It's really personal," she says.

While Carol's intention is to use only Island-grown grapes, she has built a considerable following as well for wines made totally or partially from Okanagan grapes. Her initial 45 cases of a 2005 Merlot/Cabernet Sauvignon blend was the first wine to be sold out in the wine shop. She continues to get those grapes, along with Chardonnay, which has been blended effectively with Island-grown Auxerrois.

A recent addition to her vineyard should provide the option to make an Island red. She has planted eight rows of a red Swiss hybrid. Formerly just identified with the plant breeder's number, it has been christened Labelle.

MY PICKS

The Ortega/Auxerrois blend is a tangy expression of coastal grapes. The Chardonnay/ Auxerrois blend combines Okanagan and Island fruit in a refreshing, peachy wine. Both the Merlot and the Merlot/ Cabernet blend are full of flavour.

ENRICO WINERY & VINEYARDS

For the next few years, visitors to Enrico Winery need to keep an eye open for the occasional gravel truck (seven or eight a day) grinding past the 6-hectare (15-acre) vineyard and the wine shop. Those trucks represent future vineyard. When the gravel deposit at the rear of this 20-hectare (50-acre) farm is exhausted, that slope will be contoured and prepared for more vines. If it all goes to plan, this will become one of the largest vineyards in the Cowichan Valley.

Victoria businessman Harry Smith purchased the farm in 2000 for livestock. When he discovered "there is not much money in cattle," he planted vines on the front half of the farm in 2007 and 2008, with the gravel operations supporting the development of a winery.

He had come to wine through hockey. Born in Trail, he played defence with the 1961 world champion Trail Smoke Eaters, and later with the Detroit Red Wings and several editions of Team Canada. In the early 1980s, he coached the Swiss national hockey team, living with a winery owner near Lausanne and picking grapes one vintage. "He was one of the champion wine tasters in Switzerland," Harry remembers. "I spent a lot of time with him."

There once was not much money in hockey either. Offered a playing salary he thought inadequate, Harry walked away from a Red Wings camp in the early 1960s to build an entrepreneurial career, in hotels and real estate, including shopping centres on Vancouver Island and a coffee plantation in Hawaii. His company, Columbia Fuels, is the largest petroleum products distributor on Vancouver Island. "I've done very well in business as well as in sports," says Harry, who has been inducted into sports halls of fame in both Penticton and Kelowna.

Guided by consultants and vineyard managers, Harry has planted varieties appropriate for the climate: Pinot Gris, Pinot Noir (planted in 2007), Ortega and two Blattner reds, Cabernet Libre and Cabernet Foch

SARAH COSMAN AND BUSINESS ADVISOR FRANK EDGELL

(planted in 2008). In Enrico's first vintage, Sarah Cosman, mentored by winemaker husband Daniel, made Pinot Gris and Pinot Noir from estate-grown grapes and Maréchal Foch and a Bordeaux blend from purchased fruit. The winery is counting on its Blattner reds to make big reds in coming years. Cabernet Libre, Sarah says, is so deep in colour that it "stains the glass and stains the teeth."

OPENED 2010

3280 Telegraph Road
Mill Bay, BC V0R 2P3

T 250.733.2356
W www.enricowinery.com

WHEN TO VISIT
Open 11 am – 5 pm Wednesday
to Sunday, April through October

The winery name is the Spanish equivalent of Henry, Harry's given name. It seems it was suggested by his Mexican-born wife, Maru. She is a realtor and a marketer, and Harry hopes that she will look after marketing the wines. "It's a business, if you are going to do it right, not a hobby," Harry says of the wine business. "You have to devote a lot of time to it. And I don't have much time to devote to it. I am hoping one of my grandchildren will take an interest in this place, so I can leave it to them."

MY PICKS

The silver medal–winning Pinot Grigio is crisp and tangy. Barrel samples of the Maréchal Foch, Pinot Noir and a Malbec/Merlot blend were all promising.

GLENTERRA VINEYARDS

A great deal of passion has been invested in this vineyard and winery. The original vines, a modest test block perhaps an acre in size but crowded with varieties, were planted by the legendary John Harper, a viticultural pioneer. This was his second Island vineyard. He was 74 when he began carving it from a forested property just off the Island Highway (Highway 19). A decade later, in 1998, in failing health, he sold it to John Kelly and Ruth Luxton. They were in awe at what he had launched. "John and I said if we can accomplish as much in 10 years as that old man did, we'll be happy" Ruth once said. They have, in fact, accomplished a great deal more.

Born in Glasgow in 1955, John Kelly has had a passion about wine since the 1970s—Spanish wines when his funds were tight, classified growths from Bordeaux and wines from California when he could afford to drink quality. He ran a sign-making company in Vancouver but that did not engage his interest nearly as much as the California wineries that he had begun to visit. He considered enrolling in winemaking at the University of California in 1995, found that too expensive and instead was one of the first graduates of Okanagan College's winemaking program. He and Ruth, a chef, began looking for a wine growing property and found John Harper's Cobble Hill farm.

They planted cool-climate varieties such as Pinot Noir, Pinot Blanc, Pinot Gris and Gewürztraminer while buying Okanagan grapes for the winery's initial vintage in 1999. Now that the vineyard is producing fully, most of the wines are estate-grown. However, John has continued to buy Okanagan grapes, in part a defence against the Island's variable climate and in part because John likes big reds.

The Harper legacy survives in a red blend called Brio and a white blend called Vivace, wines that rely on the potpourri of about 40 varieties that John and Ruth found in the test block when they bought the

JOHN KELLY

property. Vivace includes Pinot Blanc, Müller-Thurgau, Ortega, Bacchus, Pinot Gris, Siegerrebe, Schönburger, Auxerrois, Chasselas, Ehrenfelser, Muscat, Würzer, Huxelrebe, Regent, Gloria and Reichensteiner. Brio includes an equal list of eccentric varieties. Initially, John intended to pull out most of the oddballs until deciding it would be tragic to sacrifice mature vines when he could craft good blends.

Thistles Café lets Ruth follow her passion. She has worked as a chef in several restaurants in Vancouver and on Vancouver Island, and she has been a partner in several catering companies. Thistles is her attractive vineyard bistro and the base of a catering business.

OPENED 2000

3897 Cobble Hill Road
Cobble Hill, BC V0R 1L5
T 250.743.2330
W www.glenterravineyards.com

WHEN TO VISIT
Open 11:30 am – 5 pm Friday
to Monday, April through
September; check website for
winter hours

RESTAURANT
Thistles Café in the Vineyard
Open 11:30 am – 3 pm and
5:30 pm – 8 pm Thursday to
Sunday; check website for
winter hours

MY PICKS

Brio and Vivace must be tasted because there are no blends quite like these anywhere else. Mainstream palates will enjoy the estate-grown Pinot Gris, Pinot Blanc, Gewürztraminer and Pinot Noir as well as Merlot and Pinot Noir from Okanagan grapes. Most of the wines are made with organic grapes.

GODFREY-BROWNELL VINEYARDS

The road into the Godfrey-Brownell tasting room includes two gates, a single track through forest (watch out for an oncoming vehicle), and a bumpy drive past undisciplined vineyards. It has the feel of visiting a Kentucky moonshiner. Don't be surprised to find a bluegrass band on the patio at this entertaining, if eccentric, winery.

David Godfrey, who runs this winery with Ellen, his wife, is one of the most complex individuals among Vancouver Island vintners. He is the retired head of the University of Victoria's English department, a former publisher and the winner in 1970 of the Governor General's Award for fiction. He and Ellen also established a pioneering Internet service provider and a software company in Victoria. But farming has been in his blood since his grandparents homesteaded in Saskatchewan. David, who was born in Winnipeg in 1938, raised cattle on a farm north of Toronto before moving to Victoria in 1978. Two decades later, it was back to the land with this Cowichan Valley property.

While he is hardly a moonshiner, he started making wine before he was of legal drinking age, growing up in an enclave of Italian home winemakers who imported Zinfandel grapes by the carload every fall. The Godfreys spent about five years looking for suitable property until, in 1998, they bought 24 hectares (59 acres) just next to Dennis Zanatta's pioneering Cowichan Valley vineyard. In an amazing coincidence, David discovered a family connection to this land. The property had been settled in 1886 by a homesteader called Aaron Brownell. "He was my grandmother's second cousin," David says. "So we felt we had to put the Brownell in the winery name."

The first five hectares (12½ acres) were planted in 1999; subsequent development has taken the vineyard to nearly eight hectares (20 acres). Varieties grown include Bacchus, Pinot Gris, Chardonnay, Pinot Noir, Gamay Noir and Maréchal Foch. In 2006 he bought a four-hectare (10-acre) vineyard on nearby Mount Prevost, now called Basking Turtle, which had been planted with Gewürztraminer, Pinot Noir and Pinot Gris a few years earlier by a Vancouver doctor. The vineyards also include an eclectic mix of other varieties, along with cover crops to add nitrogen to the soils as David explores ways of moving beyond the wine industry's usual monoculture. He also intends to plant olive trees. Most of the property, however, remains in its natural state.

David's background explains the literary references on some of his wine labels (Colette, Scarlatti Sisters, Winston's Solera). The winery's big red, a blend of Maréchal Foch and Gamay, is called William Maltman Double Red. It sounds literary but it is actually named after a favourite relative who taught him how to drink, or so the story goes.

David often presides over the patio or the wine shop, adding his particular thespian touch, which makes Godfrey-Brownell a popular stop in the Island's wine tours. The welcome is relaxed and the picnic tables are freely available, even to parties arriving with their own

OPENED 2000

4911 Marshall Road
Duncan, BC V9L 6T3

T 250.715.0504

W www.gbvineyards.com

WHEN TO VISIT
Open daily noon – 5 pm
February 1 through December
24 (to 6 pm summer weekends);
by appointment from December
25 to January 31

PICNIC PATIO

DAVE GODFREY

CONTINUED NEXT PAGE...

GODFREY-BROWNELL VINEYARDS

CONTINUED

picnics, as happens from time to time. David happily sells them a glass or two, even a bottle or two, of whatever Godfrey-Brownell wine they prefer to drink. The iconic sparkling blackberry wine, a favourite at the winery's weekend brunches, is sold only at the wine shop.

"We try to give everybody that wants it the winemaker's tour," he says. "Take them in and let them taste what's in the barrel, not just what's in the bottle. It's fascinating because you are running 6,000 to 7,000 people a year through your winery, tasting wine at different stages. That's the best kind of market research you can possibly do. There is almost no relationship between what consumers like in wine and what the experts say they should like. It is quite amazing. The wine experts are a very small subset of the human population."

MY PICKS

Among the whites, I like the Bacchus, the Pinot Grigio and both the unoaked Chardonnay and the lightly oaked Chardonnay. The Pinot Noirs from 2009, a fine Island vintage, are among the winery's best. Maltman Double Red is appealingly rustic.

MALAHAT ESTATE WINERY

What could be a more scenic winery location than one near the 352-metre (1,155-foot) summit of the well-travelled Malahat Drive north of Victoria? This winery's vineyard is at half that elevation, making it still one of the highest on Vancouver Island. The 30-degree slopes are now too challenging for winery owner Lorne Tomalty, who was born in 1923. No grapes were picked in 2010 (a difficult vintage anyway). With Lorne's health an issue, the future is uncertain for a winery that fulfilled a dream late in his remarkable life.

OPENED 2005

1197 Aspen Road
Malahat, BC V0R 2L0
T 250.474.5129

WHEN TO VISIT
By appointment

LORNE TOMALTY

Born in Ottawa, he spent World War II as an armoured corps officer. Upon being discharged, he enrolled in economics and political science at the University of British Columbia. When he tried to enter the job market in 1949, his education attracted two offers: one as an airline ticket agent and the other as an insurance salesman. So he worked as a miner in the Yukon until he could afford to return to university for a master's degree in public administration.

Upon graduation in 1952, he joined the British Columbia government as a personnel assistant. By the time he retired in 1985, he had become what he calls the government's "czar of manpower." He and his wife, Peggy, a nurse, bought a 4.6-hectare (11-acre) property on the Malahat Drive. After clearing some trees, he began planting vines in 1995, choosing Ortega, Pinot Gris and Pinot Noir for this cool, high-elevation vineyard. CONTINUED NEXT PAGE...

MALAHAT ESTATE WINERY

CONTINUED

Lorne's interest in wine arose from years of making wine at home with friends of Italian heritage. His initial winery application was filed in 1997. Ironically, the civil service he had once worked with managed to lose the paperwork. Later he concluded this was good fortune because his preparations then were still premature. "I'm an Irishman," he chuckles. His forebears came from Ireland five generations ago. "The luck must still be there." The second application, filed six years later, was approved. He had begun to make wine, with Glenterra's John Kelly as his mentor, and he converted a large double garage on the property to accommodate the winery and tasting room.

Malahat vineyard's whites are crisp, reflecting the cool site that gets the morning but not the evening sun. The grapes certainly ripen adequately, especially in a warm year like 2003, when the Ortega in particular delivered good sugars and moderate acidity. As well, the Pinot Noir has surprised Lorne with good colour to match the fruitiness. With more vines coming into production, he was able to make three barrels of Pinot Noir in 2003. However, since Pinot Noir is relatively light-bodied, in 2006 Lorne addressed the demand for a big red wine by buying Merlot grapes from a South Okanagan grower. He was so impressed with the quality that he ordered more Merlot in 2008. The superb 2009 vintage on the Island yielded quality grapes from his own vineyard.

Those 2009 wines remained to be bottled a year later. Because of Lorne's health, the winery tasting room was seldom open in 2010. In spite of his personal difficulties, Lorne's optimism remains indomitable.

MY PICKS

Current range not tasted.

MERRIDALE ESTATE CIDERY

In the two decades since opening, Merridale has evolved from a rustic producer of authentic cider in a 5.2-hectare (13-acre) orchard of rare cider apple trees to a must-stop destination, with a year-round restaurant, a spa, a "relaxation" patio and a brandy house. Two yurts, overlooking a boardwalk around a pond, are available for various social events. In 2010, about two dozen weddings were held at Merridale. This all speaks to the imagination and the business acumen with which Rick Pipes and Janet Docherty turned a struggling cidery into a viable business since buying it in 2000.

Merridale was incorporated in 1987 by Albert Piggott, a retired Scottish teacher. He pursued his lifelong cider passion after he moved to southern Vancouver Island in 1954 and found that the climate and the soils compared well to England's best cider regions. He opened the cidery in 1992. English cider tastes quite different from the big volume ciders in British Columbia, which are made with dessert apples. Switching consumer palates proved to be a major challenge for Al. Soon, he was seeking investors or buyers for the business. Rick and Janet arrived with a purchase offer in the nick of time. "We were Al's last ditch," Rick says. "He was already prepared to shut it down when we came along and started negotiating with him."

"When our four-year-old was born," Rick told me in a 2003 interview, "Janet had been doing commercial real estate for a number of years and I had been practising law [in Victoria] for

OPENED 1992

1230 Merridale Road, RR1
Cobble Hill, BC V0R 1L0

T   250.743.4293
    1.800.998.9908 (toll free)

W   www.merridalecider.com

WHEN TO VISIT
Open daily 10:30 am – 5:30 pm

RESTAURANT
La Pommeraie Bistro
Reservations recommended

CONTINUED NEXT PAGE...

MERRIDALE ESTATE CIDERY

CONTINUED

about fifteen years. Janet didn't want to go back to real estate and said, 'let's start looking for a business.' We looked for two years." They came upon the cidery by chance, when one of Rick's clients considered buying Merridale, only to have the deal fall through. Rick and Janet concluded this turnaround opportunity was the business they were looking for.

"Right from the beginning, our business plan was based on the need to increase traffic to the valley," Rick says. They joined the Wine Islands Vintners Association; for a time, Janet volunteered as president of the association, contributing her considerable entrepreneurial energy to the common needs of all the Cowichan Valley's producers. "It's way easier to market 15 wineries than it is to market one little cidery," Rick says. Over time, Merridale has become a leading attraction.

Learning to make cider was Rick's initial challenge. The cider maker who had been working with Al had died in a car crash late in 1999; and Al went to New Zealand shortly after selling Merridale. "Although I have a commerce degree and I am a lawyer, I originally wanted to go into something that was more science-related," Rick says. His university-level science courses, including microbiology, equipped him to understand fermentation. He located cider consultants in Britain who, through the Internet, helped him navigate through problems.

There is no doubt he learned his new craft well. Product variation is a thing of the past. The ciders are fresh in flavour, even including Scrumpy, the most rustic of all the ciders. The origin of the name is "scrump," a term for stealing cider apples. Rick and Janet disliked the taste of Merridale's original Scrumpy and wanted to discontinue the product until discovering it had its fans. Rick reformulated the product, and managed to satisfy its traditional customers while achieving flavours he likes.

RICK PIPES AND JANET DOCHERTY

Rick took the art one step further by importing an elegant German still and making distilled products from apples and blackberries that Merridale calls Oh de Vie. He has also made a Calvados-style apple brandy but, to date, this product has not been offered for sale. "It is a completely unprofitable business," says Janet (who has a Mexican uncle who produces tequila). The problem: onerous provincial taxes on distilled products. If and when those taxes become more reasonable, Merridale will start selling its Cowichan Apple Brandy.

MY PICKS

Scrumpy is a cider that Merridale believes Scotch drinkers will appreciate. Traditional is so true to authentic English cider that it won an award in a competition at the Hereford Cider Museum. Both it and House Cider, a pub draft, are dry. Merri Berri, Cyser and Winter Apple are dessert ciders. Pomme Oh! and Mure Oh! are 19 percent fortified apple and blackberry beverages, finished off-dry. Apple Oh de Vie, at 40 percent, is a clean tasting apple *eau de vie*. Blackberry Oh de Vie is as delicious as a quality gin.

MUSE ESTATE WINERY

Peter and Jane Ellman took over Chalet Estate Winery in the spring of 2008, just as the economic slowdown put the brakes on booming sales of British Columbia wine. However, confident in their strong sales background, they doubled production that fall to 3,800 cases, and bumped it up again to 4,400 cases in 2009. At least half of the wine is sold directly from the winery, reinvigorated with a new name, a popular bistro and daringly brash wine labels. It has been a while since the sleepy Saanich Peninsula has seen this much energy.

The bistro comes from Peter's first career as a chef. Born in Wisconsin, he worked on private yachts after chef's school before moving to the restaurant business. He ran a fine French restaurant in Baton Rouge, Louisiana, for four years. In 1984, when a downturn in the oil industry hurt that city's economy, he switched to selling California wines from a base in Texas. He also networked with some leading winemakers, among them Sonoma vintner Kent Rosenblum. "He and I used to be rollerblade partners at the Aspen food and wine festival," Peter recalls. "We were the team that would beat everybody. I was much skinnier back then." Since buying the Saanich winery, Peter has tapped his contacts for advice and support.

Jane Ellman's background brings the hospitality industry touch to running the wine shop. A native of Edmonton, she spent 16 years as a general manager with the Marriott hotel chain in the United States. Her father had founded a successful manufacturer of oil drilling equipment. When he decided to retire, Peter and Jane returned to Canada to run the business. Peter put his marketing skills to work and sales rose tenfold. "I made the phone ring," says Peter. "That's what I do." But, as Jane says, their heart was not in selling drilling rig mats.

They had wanted a winery for about 10 years and looked as far afield as New Zealand. They were close to buying an Oliver-area vine-

JANE AND PETER ELLMAN

yard when Jane learned, in an Internet search, that Chalet was available. "We didn't know about Island wineries," she says. They were utterly charmed by the Saanich Peninsula. "We knew immediately that this was where we wanted to spend the rest of our lives. It is so fantastic."

Chalet had been established by Michael Betts, a former British submarine officer, and Linda Plimley, a member of a pioneering Victoria automotive family. In the 1980s, they purchased a pastoral forested property at the top end of the Saanich Peninsula, across the road from the storied Deep Cove Chalet restaurant. They considered growing walnuts or farming trout but, inspired by other new vineyards on the peninsula, planted Ortega, Bacchus and Pinot Gris in the 1.2-hectare (three-acre) vineyard in 1998 and opened the winery three years later.

The Ellmans stamped their own personalities on the winery by changing the name and adopting brashly provocative labels in 2009. Peter called the winery Muse as a tribute to Jane—his muse, he says—who had inspired a

OPENED 2001
(AS CHALET ESTATE)

11195 Chalet Road
North Saanich, BC V8L 5M1

T   250.656.2552

W www.musewinery.ca

WHEN TO VISIT
Open 11 am – 5 pm Tuesday to Sunday May through September; noon – 5 pm Thursday to Saturday and 1 pm – 5 pm Sunday during winter

RESTAURANT
Muse Bistro
Open Thursday to Sunday during summer

CONTINUED NEXT PAGE...

MUSE ESTATE WINERY

CONTINUED

label designer to create the mermaid image on the new labels. The saucy back labels came from a focus group that brainstormed during one of Peter's barbecued pork dinners. The Pinot Gris, for example, describes itself as "a festive giddy gal with lots of snappy one-liners" and playfully provides flavour descriptors and food pairings. The new labels caused an immediate jump in sales.

Muse now draws grapes from several Saanich vineyards. "But you know, I like making wine from all the varietals that I enjoy drinking," Peter says. That includes Viognier and Bordeaux reds grown in the Okanagan, where they flourish in a climate more reliable than Vancouver Island. "This is a business," Peter says. "I am not going to gamble on weather."

MY PICKS

The refreshing crispness of Bacchus, Ortega and the Pinot Gris are good expressions of Saanich terroir. Maréchal Foch is a full-bodied Island red. Fumé Blanc, Viognier, Grande Dame Rouge and Syrah are full, rich wines from Okanagan terroir.

ROCKY CREEK WINERY

The olive trees planted here in 2010 are the latest step on Mark and Linda Holford's remarkable career path from working in a Sarnia refinery to growing artisanal wine on Vancouver Island. Mark, the third generation in his family to make wine at home, realized a long-held dream when he turned winemaking into his profession in 2005.

"Ever since I was in my early teens, I helped my dad make wine," Mark recounts. "He did a lot of amateur winemaking, and my grandfather in England did a lot." That skill made him popular at university, when he agreed to make wine and beer for his friends as well. It dawned on him that this "could be something I could do as an occupation."

Born in Deep River, Ontario, in 1968, Mark is a chemical engineer with a master's degree in environmental engineering. He met Linda in Calgary, her hometown, when he was completing a co-operative studies assignment with an oil company. She is an engineering technologist with management skills gained in the oil industry. They spent two and a half years in Sarnia where Mark worked in the Shell petrochemical plant.

"But we always wanted to come to Vancouver Island," says Linda. "When we were in Calgary, we wanted to get a job [here] and an opportunity happened first in Sarnia." In the fall of 2001, Mark and Linda were vacationing in Victoria, where Linda's retired parents lived, when he found a position at the pulp mill at Crofton. They bought a home nearby in Ladysmith. Plans for a CONTINUED NEXT PAGE...

OPENED 2005

1854 Myhrest Road
Cowichan. Bay. BC V0R 1N1

T 250.748.5622

W www.rockycreekwinery.ca

WHEN TO VISIT
Open 11 am – 4 pm Thursday to Sunday. April through mid-September; 11 am – 4 pm Friday and Saturday. mid-September through mid-December; otherwise by appointment

PICNIC AREA

ROCKY CREEK WINERY

winery were put on hold because there was no room for a vineyard on their suburban street. Then they discovered they could get a commercial licence and make wine with purchased grapes. Rocky Creek opened in 2005, making 600 cases, with grapes from a vineyard at Chemainus and purchased wild blackberries. Their first release was a port-style blackberry wine—which also won the winery its first medal.

Linda and Mark, who continues to work as an environmental consultant, soon figured out that small wineries are more profitable with a land-based licence (because the government takes much less in taxes and charges). In the winter of 2008, they moved to a three-hectare (7½-acre) farm in the Cowichan Valley, on a property almost back to back with Venturi Schulze Vineyards.

They now manage the Chemainus vineyard, growing Ortega, Siegerrebe, Bacchus, Pinot Gris and Pinot Noir. They also manage a small Cowichan Valley vineyard planted with Pinot Noir, Pinot Gris and several other white varieties. They buy grapes from another nearby vineyard which grows, among other varieties, some Tempranillo grapes. In their own Cowichan Valley vineyard, they had planted Maréchal Foch, some of Valentin Blattner's Swiss hybrids, and almost a hectare (2½ acres) of blackberries.

The cultivated blackberries are required by the regulations for land-based wineries, however ridiculous it is to plant more blackberries, given the abundance of wild blackberries on Vancouver Island. Mark has made a trial lot of sparkling blackberry wine and expects to increase that production.

Rocky Creek's wines include two named for Mark and Linda's daughters—Robin's Rosé for their eldest daughter and Katherine's Sparkle for their younger daughter. The rosé is made with Pinot Noir, a variety for which Mark is developing an affinity. The sparkling wine was first made

LINDA AND MARK HOLFORD

in 2008, as an innovative cuvée of Gewürztraminer, Ortega and Bacchus with a crisp, dry finish.

It will be a few years before Rocky Creek can also make olive oil. Five trees were planted in 2010 (Mark and Linda already had two). "After we make sure they survive our winters in Cowichan Bay, we will get more," Mark says. "We would like a small grove of 30 to 40 trees. Production is not likely for at least five years."

MY PICKS

Both the Pinot Gris and the Ortega are delicious, especially in great vintages like 2009. The rosé and the Pinot Noir have a track record for being well crafted. Katherine's Sparkle makes a good case for Island-grown sparkling wines. The blackberry's flavours are true to tastes of the fresh berries. Ask the winery for cocktail suggestions—such as Mûre Royale, with one ounce of blackberry wine and three ounces of sparkling wine.

SASKATOON BERRY FARM & SOUTH ISLAND WINES

The Canadian distance record for shooting the stopper from a bottle of sparkling wine is 98 feet (just under 30 metres), according to Gord Graziano. It came about when an early batch of his saskatoon berry sparkling wine had too much pressure to be marketed safely. "You could blow a hole in the kitchen ceiling," he warns. Now that he has refined the process, he makes a wine with a safe two atmospheres of pressure.

How Gord came to make these wines, including one as explosive as a small gun, is quite a tale. Born in Toronto in 1946 and trained as a commercial designer, he met his future wife, Valerie, an Edmonton lawyer, during a Banff vacation. Gord never moved back to Toronto, instead pursuing a career as an art consultant within Edmonton schools and with private clients.

About four decades ago, he began making wines at home in St. Albert, an Edmonton suburb, and the hobby soon grew bigger than he had planned. "It started as a combined family thing—Italian families making it together," he recalls. "That's how I got going. We would make the wine centrally and split it among the families. The wine was so popular that it was difficult to stop people from asking for it. I thought it was time to get commercial."

But when Gord applied for a winery licence, he found nothing but regulatory roadblocks in his way. He was told that he needed to make 250,000 litres a year to qualify, when all he wanted to do was a few thousand litres for his friends, legally. "The bottom line was that the whole industry in Alberta was controlled by two or three players," Gord concluded. "They didn't want little wineries like me around." In 1997, Gord and Valerie gave up on unsympathetic regulators (and Edmonton winters) to move to the Cowichan Valley.

Gord hoped to work with one of the valley's wineries, a plan derailed by a heart attack, a stroke and the loss of much of his sight. Normally cheerful, he was plunged into deep depression until, at a family member's suggestion, he planted a therapeutic vineyard in the backyard of his Cobble Hill home. "It started out as a make-work project, but once you get into it, you get interested in physiology of the grapes, the soil sciences, weather, so it became kind of an obsession for a few years," he says. Soon, his life was focused on 300 vines in 17 mani-cured rows. Rather than planting what everyone else was growing, he stub-bornly planted the varieties he likes to drink: Cabernet Sauvignon, Merlot and Cabernet Franc. In some years, these varieties are not ripe enough to pick. In other years, he makes light wines. In a rare hot vintage like 2002, he has made a more than credible Cabernet Sauvignon. Fortunately, he and Valerie prefer wines light enough that they can be enjoyed throughout the day.

The vineyard revived his dream of creating a winery. He incorporated South Island Vineyard and Winery. Then he enlisted a partner, Al Dyrland, a former Albertan who, with his wife, Connie, has run Vancouver Island's only

OPENED 2009

1245 Fisher Road
Cobble Hill. BC V0R 1L4
T 250.743.1189

WHEN TO VISIT
Open daily 10 am – 5 pm

GORD GRAZIANO

CONTINUED NEXT PAGE...

SASKATOON BERRY FARM & SOUTH ISLAND WINES

CONTINUED

saskatoon berry farm since the late 1990s. The farm's 3.3 hectares (eight acres) of berry bushes draw a clientele nostalgic about the berries of their Prairie childhood. Al and Connie were already selling jams and pies from the farm store and added wine in 2009.

Al had approached Gord to make wine from sweet, raisin-like berries left behind by the U-pick clients. Not happy with the saskatoon berry wine, Gord hit upon a blend of his red grape wine with the dark saskatoon juice, refermented with Champagne yeast in stainless steel drums. This secondary fermentation creates the bubbles in the wines. "To me, it is celebratory," Gord says. "You are celebrating with a sparkling wine."

MY PICKS

There are only two wines, both sparkling blends of red wine and saskatoon wine—Luck Be a Lady and the slightly sweeter Grandmother's Recipe. Neither is overly sweet, just sweet enough for the demographic that patronizes the shop at the berry farm.

SEA CIDER FARM & CIDERHOUSE

It is not a coincidence that Sea Cider's tasting room has the rustic ambiance of an English pub. Kristen Jordan, who operates this cidery with husband Bruce, got her taste for cider while studying at a college in Wales in 1985. "There was a small pub on campus and there were small pubs in two of the nearby villages," she remembers. "You could have a glass of cider, a half pint, enough to be social. That sociability was one of the things that encouraged us to build this cider house [as] a welcoming place where people can enjoy a drink together."

Raised in Medicine Hat, Kristen first worked as an international consultant after studying economics at McGill. She spent three years on Ethiopian agriculture projects. "All my mother's side are farmers and ranchers," she explains. When civil war flared up in Ethiopia, she went to France to study economic geography and then, after a brief return to Ethiopia, did post-graduate work at Yale on food security issues. She worked several years for the United Nations before joining a Victoria consulting firm. In that city she met Bruce, a lawyer and former rugby

OPENED 2007

2487 Mount St. Michael Road
Saanichton, BC V8M 1T7

T 250.544.4824

W www.seacider.ca

WHEN TO VISIT
Open 11 am – 6 pm Wednesday
to Sunday and on holiday
Mondays

KRISTEN JORDAN

CONTINUED NEXT PAGE...

SEA CIDER FARM & CIDERHOUSE

player. After a lengthy search for a cider property, they found a former sheep farm on the Saanich Peninsula with a view eastward to the Haro Strait. They planted 50 varieties of apples on four hectares (10 acres) and built a cidery in 2006. Kristen and Bruce, who no longer practises law, immersed themselves in the craft of cider by taking courses at Washington State University.

In the organic orchards that support their cider production, Kristen and Bruce grow about 60 apple varieties. "You are probably not as interested in apples as I am," she suggests. "It's all that I think about and all that I talk about." Her passion for apples began in her teens, when she inherited a Shuswap orchard that is still growing heritage varieties for Sea Cider. Only a cider fanatic would recognize the strange varieties, generally European in origin, which bear names such as Belle de Boskoop, Bill's Red Flesh, Brown Snout, Greensleeves, King of Tomkins and Yarlington Mill.

"The European apples give you quite an earthy, full-bodied cider, like a very big beer or a tannic wine," Kristen explains. "The [heritage] North American apples give you more of a crisp and clean, high-acid product, like a really dry, acidic Riesling with quite a fruity nose." That aptly describes her effervescent cider, called Kings & Spies; one of the varieties is Northern Spy.

Certain ciders, notably Rumrunner (a semi-dry sparkling cider) derive character from aging in barrels. "Some cider makers in the UK use old Scotch barrels," says Kristen, who learned this when she researched cider history. After a British cider consultant advised her to find rum barrels, she bought barrels in which the Newfoundland & Labrador Liquor Corporation aged a rum called Screech. Those barrels are no longer available, so Sea Cider now buys used bourbon barrels, seasoning them with rum before aging cider in them.

Sea Cider's products are packaged in glass bottles like wine. "Typically in the US and in Canada, you find cider in beer bottles," Kristen says. "It kind of gets plunked in with beer, and it really has much more in common with wine than with beer." The other advantage of glass, she notes, is that ciders can be aged to develop additional complexity in the bottles. "This whole thing is about resurrecting a lost tradition," Kristen says of cider making.

MY PICKS

There is something for every palate here, notably Flagship, a dry, unsulphured cider and the ultra-dry Wild English. Kings & Spies and Pippins are both slightly off-dry and Rumrunner is a robust sparkling cider. Those preferring sweet ciders will be delighted with Cyser or Pommeau, two aperitif ciders, or Pomona, a dessert cider.

SILVERSIDE FARM & WINERY

During 30 years of growing berries, Silverside Farm established a reputation as one of Cobble Hill's best blueberry producers. When the farm and the winery came on the market in 2009, one of its steady customers, Lyn Jakimchuk, bought it in partnership with her husband Don Bull.

The farm is named for the silver birch trees planted along the driveway by Bill and Jean Aten after they bought the property in 1982. "My idea was that we could have a mixed farm," said Jean, a former teacher. With Bill working as an engineer with the Ministry of Forests, she found the workload was too heavy. "We were both getting worn out, after milking five cows morning and night," she recalled. On the advice of an agriculture expert, they switched from livestock to blueberries and raspberries. They succeeded as berry growers and Jean had time to develop her skills as an artist.

In 2004, a local home winemaker, Harold Moulton, persuaded Jean and Bill to start a winery. "It sounded quite exclusive," Jean laughed later. With Harold and then Bill making the wines, Silverside opened its tasting room with wines from blueberries, raspberries and blackberries. Later, a rare tayberry wine was added, along with port-style berry wines.

When Bill and Jean decided to retire, Silverside also sounded exclusive to Lyn and Don. Like Jean, Lyn is a former teacher who was looking for a change from that high-pressure career. "I looked at the teachers in the staff room that were totally burned out and asked, 'Do I want to be here in 10 years?'" she says. "I still have education in my heart. I would like to have students here on field trips and have informal learning going on."

Don is an investment advisor who finds time to make wine and manage the cellar in the afternoons, when the stock markets are closed. "This is a much nicer office to work in," he says of the winery. Silverside

LYN JAKIMCHUK AND DON BULL

continues to offer its familiar range of berry wines—robust wines with 15 to 18 percent alcohol and gobs of flavour. Don and Lyn have added jams, jellies and yogurt cones to their offerings. As well, they now have two miniature horses, to be trained for wagon rides around this bucolic farm.

MY PICKS

The Tayberry wine, a seldom-seen fruit wine, is exotically spicy with a dry finish. The Wild Blackberry wine is full-bodied and rich in berry flavours. The Raspberry Dessert Wine has intense aromas and flavours and pairs superbly with chocolate.

OPENED 2005

3810 Cobble Hill Road
Cobble Hill, BC V0R 1L0

T 250.743.9149
   1.877.743.9149 (toll free)

W www.silversidefarm.com

WHEN TO VISIT
Open daily 10 am – 6 pm June through September; 11 am – 4 pm Saturday, October through May

STARLING LANE WINERY

When it comes to winemaking, John Wrinch has a perfectionist's attitude. His 2009 Ortega is an outstanding example, showcasing that variety's lifted aromatics and tangy flavours so reminiscent of a fine New Zealand Sauvignon Blanc. It is startling, then, that John says he is not entirely happy with the wine. He thinks he could improve its complexity by blending in a small percentage, say 10 percent, of another white. He brings that diamond-polishing attitude to the production of all Starling Lane wines, and it certainly shows.

It all begins in the vineyards that grow Starling Lane's grapes. In the early 1990s three couples each planted small but impeccably managed vineyards near each other on the Saanich Peninsula. Jerry and Sherry Mussio may have set all this motion when—because Jerry is Italian by way of Trail and likes to make his own wine—they planted a few vines on their hobby sheep farm. John Wrinch, a radiologist who had become a home winemaker while practising in Kamloops, bought a lamb, saw the vines, and decided to plant grapes on his property. Independently, Ken and Sue Houston had planted vines already and were winning awards in amateur wine competitions for their Maréchal Foch.

The three grape growers had all been considering opening wineries but each has only about a hectare of vines. When they recognized shared ambitions in 2003, they decided to partner in a single winery at John and Jacqueline Wrinch's farm, an attractive property rich in history. It was acquired in 1859 by Judge Matthew Baillie Begbie, remembered today, unfairly perhaps, as the Hanging Judge. A British lawyer, he had come to what is now British Columbia in 1858 to help dispense law during the Fraser Gold Rush. He would spend 35 years as chief justice, during which he seems to have handed down relatively few death sentences (which were mandatory in murder convictions). The partners at Starling Lane thought about calling it the Hanging Judge Winery. Not only did the

JACQUELINE AND JOHN WRINCH, SHERRY AND JERRY MUSSICO
AND SUE AND KEN HOUSTON (PHOTO BY QUINTON GORDON)

whimsy not appeal to them; they speculated that descendants of some of the few who did hang might be offended.

The vineyards cultivated by the partners complement each other. On their Heritage Farm Vineyard, as the Wrinches call it, John grows eight different varietals: Ortega, Maréchal Foch, Léon Millot, Regent, Pinot Noir, Müller Thurgau, Bacchus and Schönburger. Ken and Sue Houston, who also have a luxury bed and breakfast, grow Pinot Gris, Pinot Noir, Pinot Blanc, Gewürztraminer and Maréchal Foch on their Hummingbird Vineyard. The Mussios, no longer in the sheep business, grow Ortega, Pinot Gris and Maréchal Foch on the farm they have owned since 1993. The partners only buy from one other grower, a Cowichan Valley vineyard supplying carefully nurtured Maréchal Foch, Pinot Blanc, Pinot Noir and Chardonnay. "What the growers here have in common is a passion for the plants," Jerry says.

Starling Lane's first vintage, in 2004, was a mere 200 cases of wine. That was increased to 500 the next year. Starling Lane now produces only 1,000 cases a year and sells out quickly.

OPENED 2005

5271 Old West Saanich Road
Victoria, BC V9E 2A9

T 250.881.7422

W www.starlinglanewinery.com

WHEN TO VISIT
Open noon – 5 pm weekends,
May through September; and by
appointment

MY PICKS

I like the entire portfolio from Ortega to Blackberry. One of the most exceptional wines here is Célébration Brut, a sparkling wine that rivals Champagne.

TUGWELL CREEK HONEY FARM & MEADERY

The six meaderies in British Columbia owe a debt to Tugwell Creek's Robert Liptrot and Dana LeComte for breaking ground and winning the first meadery licence from reluctant regulators. Tugwell Creek was licensed as a fruit winery, there being no rules for honey wines. In 2002, Dana told one journalist, "We're trying to put out a product [which] they don't have written in their regulations." She had more patience in dealing with regulators than her husband, Robert, who once said he preferred being stung by bees to writing letters to bureaucrats.

Of course, he knows how to avoid bee stings. Robert, who was born in 1956 and raised in East Vancouver, has been working with bees since, at age seven, he began helping a beekeeper neighbour. Eventually, he earned a master's degree in apicultural science. After keeping a small number of hives in the Fraser Valley, he began making mead in the early 1990s.

In 1996, seeking a pristine environment in which to produce honey, Robert and Dana moved to a five-hectare (12-acre) property north of Sooke, open to the cleansing ocean breezes. "We don't get a lot of pollution," says Robert, who can see the distant Olympic Mountains from Tugwell Creek's tasting room. Vancouver Island had another advantage at the time—a quarantine that prevented importing bees from elsewhere, along with attendant disease. The quarantine has since been breached, unfortunately. Robert is tackling the same challenges that threaten beekeeping elsewhere on the continent, both by his research on bee genetics and by teaching others how to keep bees.

In a quest for exceptionally pure honey, Robert places most of his hives (about one hundred) in the logged areas of the mountain forests beyond Sooke. "There is nobody driving around up in the clearcuts," he notes. The bees gather nectar from plants flourishing there, including salal and fireweed. Depending on how generous nature is, Robert harvests between 1,800 and 2,700 kilograms (4,000 and 6,000 pounds) of honey each season. About two-thirds is used for mead; the rest is sold directly to honey lovers.

Robert describes mead as the ultimate expression of beekeeping. Mead is perhaps the oldest of civilization's fermented beverages. "When you read Chaucer's *Canterbury Tales*, they were drinking mead," Dana says. In fact, mead appears in older literature, such as Norse legends. "Rumour has it that someone's bucket of honey was left out and filled with rain water," she adds. "Honey has a lot of natural yeast in it and it fermented . . . and that is how the first mead was made."

The language of mead sounds medieval. Mead flavoured with spices or herbs is called metheglin, said to be derived from *meddyglyn*, a Welsh word meaning "medicine"—presumably because medicinal herbs were made palatable by mixing them with mead. When fruit or fruit juice is added, the mead is called melomel. There are abundant subcategories of this style. Mead made with rose petals is called rhodomel. When the fruit is apple or apple cider, the mead is called cyser. When grapes or wine are added, the mead is called pyment. These

OPENED 2003

8750 West Coast Road
Sooke, BC V9Z 1H2
T 250.642.1956
W www.tugwellcreekfarm.com

WHEN TO VISIT
Open noon – 5 pm Wednesday to Sunday, May through September; noon – 5 pm weekends, October through April; closed January

ROBERT LIPTROT

CONTINUED NEXT PAGE...

TUGWELL CREEK HONEY FARM & MEADERY

CONTINUED

styles usually are finished either as dry or slightly off-dry, contrary to the perception that honey wine is sweet. There are sweet meads, called sack. Tugwell Creek even makes a fortified mead that it calls Vintage Sac.

"All of my meads are made in a wine style," says Robert, who uses standard wine yeasts. He ages most of the meads in French oak barrels; some also finish fermentation in the oak. The time in oak is typically shorter than would be the case with wine, to prevent the wood flavours from dominating the complex taste of mead. The fruit mead, or melomel, spends almost no time in oak. "Melomels are quite a delicate wine," he explains. "We are trying to bring forward the flavours of the fruit as well as the honey and marry them together in such a way that they won't be overpowering each other." The fruit comes from Tugwell Creek's own heritage berry bushes.

Because honey contains natural preservatives, meads appeal to consumers who react against sulphur, which is often added in minimal quantities to table wines to preserve them but is unnecessary in mead.

MY PICKS

Wassail Gold is a sensual dessert mead made from a secret recipe known only to Robert and an uncle. Vintage Sac, a fortified product, is the mead world's answer to port. For dry meads that pair with food, try Tugwell Creek's Brazen Blackberry or Kickass Currant or Solstice Metheglin.

22 OAKS WINERY

Much of this property's forest was removed in 2006 so that Jeff and Lisa MacLeod could plant a vineyard and house/winery complex. A friend counted the remaining Garry Oak trees and found 22. By a remarkable coincidence, that number is special among this winery's partners. It was one person's birthday, one couple's wedding anniversary and the number on another partner's professional hockey jersey. The winery was clearly destined to be called 22 Oaks.

A career Safeway store manager (as was his father), Jeff acquired his interest in wine and winemaking from his wife's Italian family. Her father and grandfather, both called Giovanni Cosco, made a barrel or two of Zinfandel every fall and Jeff soon joined in. "We used to drink it from Mason jars right out of the barrel," he remembers. "It was as Old World as it got. But I have always had a huge science interest, so the biology of it and the microchemistry intrigued me."

The decision to open a winery was taken after several Napa Valley vacations, followed by preparing methodically with courses in winemaking. He

OPENED 2009

1 – 6380 Lakes Road
Duncan, BC V9L 5V6

T   250.709.0787

W www.22oakswinery.ca

WHEN TO VISIT
Open 11 am – 5 pm Thursday
to Sunday

PICNIC AREA

JEFF MACLEOD

CONTINUED NEXT PAGE...

22 OAKS WINERY

CONTINUED

conceived of including the winery and the tasting room in his new home after attending a seminar in the United States on small-winery design. The economical, all-in-one design has the tasting room on the ground floor, finished with lumber from the property's trees, with windows looking onto the picnic facilities and the 1.5-hectare (3.5-acre) vineyard.

The winery happens to be in the Cowichan Valley because Jeff was transferred there in 1996 to manage Duncan's Safeway. (He now commutes daily to Victoria to manage a larger store.) The partners in the winery, including two former professional hockey players, are friends that Jeff and Lisa made in the Valley.

Greg and Judy Adams live in the other house on the winery property. Now the owner of a construction company and several Tim Horton's franchises, Greg was born in Duncan in 1960 and returned to the community in 1990 after a 10-year hockey career, most of it with the Washington Capitals. Doug and Tracey Bodger live nearby. A native of Chemainus, Doug spent 16 years as an NHL defenceman. After ending his career with the Vancouver Canucks, he moved to Duncan to operate a sporting goods store and coach hockey. Sawmill owner Jerry Doman and his wife Ronnie, who have a small Pinot Noir vineyard up the road from 22 Oaks, are the fourth couple in the partnership.

The vineyards supporting 22 Oaks were planted in 2007 and 2008. In the winery block and in a small leased block next door, Jeff grows primarily Cabernet Foch (a Blattner hybrid) and Maréchal Foch, with smaller plantings of Merlot, Sauvignon Blanc and Tempranillo, the major red of Spain but a rare variety in the Cowichan Valley. Jeff was delighted when the variety produced a first tiny harvest in 2009 and the grapes reached a more than acceptable ripeness of 24 Brix. On his property, which slopes toward shallow Quamichan Lake, Jerry has three clones of Pinot Noir. "It is actually quite a good little spot facing the lake," Jeff says. "This is one of the warmest spots in the valley."

The first several vintages at 22 Oaks, 2008 and 2009, relied on grapes purchased from both the Okanagan and other Island vineyards. "Our focus is going to be 100 percent Cowichan Valley grapes in the future," Jeff says.

MY PICKS

The Syrah, Syrah Foch and Pinot Gris, with which the winery opened, made largely from Okanagan grapes, show that Jeff learned winemaking well from his wife's Italian family. In the future, look for a signature red blend, a Pinot Noir and a blackberry dessert wine.

VENTURI SCHULZE VINEYARDS

Venturi Schulze Vineyards has generally relied on word of mouth to sell the 1,500 or so cases of wine that it makes each year. The strategy has worked because the wines are always top quality. Even so, it is also a good idea to give those mouths something fresh to talk about from time to time. Thus in 2010, Giordano Venturi and his wife, Marilyn Schulze, switched to screw-capped bottles with elegantly contemporary labels. "In the old days, it wasn't that important" says Marilyn. "We purposely did understated labels. We were just stubbornly making the point that the quality is in the bottle." The quality is still there but now is in bottles that stand out on crowded wine store shelves.

Other changes occurred here as well in 2010. They released Pilastro, the winery's first off-dry white table wine, priced it just under $20 and watched it fly out the door. "We have fallen in love with it ourselves," Marilyn says. "Our preference has always been absolutely dry wines. We had noticed that there are a lot of people who will say they like a dry wine but will go for this."

The many Italian wine names here speak to the winery's heritage. Pilastro is an Italian word that means both pillar and a pile of bricks. Giordano's father was a bricklayer in a village near Maranello, where Ferrari has its factory. Another Venturi Schulze wine, a Pinot Noir rosé with piquant acidity, is called Maranello. "We said perfect, it's a Ferrari wine with its racy acidity" Marilyn explains.

Giordano, who was born in 1941, came to Canada in 1967 and became an electronics teacher. Marilyn was born in Australia in 1951, the daughter of a doctor who immigrated to Canada in 1970. With a degree in microbiology, she also became a teacher. Both found the teaching profession stressful. In 1988 they moved to this Cowichan Valley farm, refurbished the 1893 farmhouse and began planting vines.

Perfectionists by nature, they set the bar high from the start. "When

L TO R: MICHELLE SCHULZE, MARILYN SCHULZE AND GIORDANO VENTURI

we started this, it was always understood that under no circumstances would we ever spray pesticides or herbicides," Marilyn says. Compost and seaweeds fertilize the vines. Although the winery has never sought organic certification, the farming practices are organic and the wines are vegan because no animal products are used in the vineyard or the winery.

They are firmly committed to estate-grown wines, going to great lengths to produce good grapes in a challenging climate. In 1998, Venturi Schulze was the first winery on Vancouver Island to tent some of its vines. Some producers scoff at this labour-intensive procedure, but it enables Giordano and Marilyn to make some of the valley's ripest Pinot Noir. Tented grapes ripen earlier and with more sugar. In 2003, Venturi Schulze even overdid it, producing a Pinot Noir with an astonishing 15.4 percent alcohol, a good two percent above what Giordano considers ideal. The wine was so big and rich that they recommended it with game.

They also produce two unique wine-based products. Verjus is made from the

OPENED 1993

4235 Vineyard Road (Trans-Canada Highway)
Cobble Hill, BC V0R 1L5

T 250.743.5630

W www.venturischulze.com

WHEN TO VISIT
Open 10 am – 5 pm weekends and holiday Mondays, April 15 through December 31; otherwise by appointment

MARILYN SCHULZE WITH TENTED VINES

CONTINUED NEXT PAGE...

VENTURI SCHULZE VINEYARDS

CONTINUED

unfermented juice of semi-ripe grapes. It is a tangy product used in salad dressings and sauces for cooking. The other is the winery's intensely flavoured balsamic vinegar, matured in small barrels like the great balsamic vinegars of Modena. Giordano made his original barrel of vinegar in 1970 and it remains among the host of barrels in the vinegary.

MY PICKS

Everything, but especially the Brut Naturel, Pinot Noir, Pilastro, Millefiore, Bianco Di Collina, Rosso Di Collina, Terracotta, Brandenburg No. 3 and, of course, Balsamic Vinegar.

VIGNETI ZANATTA WINERY & VINEYARDS

The largest seller here is Damasco, a non-vintage white first released in 1998, a virtue arising from necessity. Husband and wife proprietors and winemakers Jim Moody and Loretta Zanatta were not too happy with their Ortega from 1996, which had been a cool growing season, and held some back to blend with the 1997. They also refreshed the fruitiness of the wine by immersing freshly pressed skins of 1997 grapes in 1996 wine. The technique was so effective that it remains the basic recipe for Damasco, with the addition of Muscat, Madeleine Sylvaner and Auxerrois to the blend. As a non-vintage wine, it can be blended to a consistent taste and style year in and year out. "Creative winemaking," Jim says.

Vigneti Zanatta anchors a 12-hectare (30-acre) vineyard, one of the largest on Vancouver Island, which began with a one-acre test plot planted in 1981 by Dennis Zanatta, Loretta's father. Dennis, who died in 2008, was a farmer's son from Treviso in northern Italy, who came to Canada in 1950. Nine years later, he bought a dairy farm near Duncan that also had a mature orchard, suggesting that grapes might also thrive

OPENED 1992

5039 Marshall Road, RR3
Duncan, BC V9L 6S3

T 250.748.2338

W www.zanatta.ca

WHEN TO VISIT
Call for seasonal hours

RESTAURANT
Vinoteca on the Vineyard
Open noon – 3 pm Wednesday
to Sunday during summer

T 250.709.2279

CONTINUED NEXT PAGE...

VIGNETI ZANATTA WINERY & VINEYARDS

CONTINUED

on the property. Over the following decade, he expanded the vineyard, took part in a government-sponsored grape-growing trial (the Duncan Project), sent Loretta to wine school in Italy and launched a family winery. It was the first commercial winery to start on Vancouver Island in 65 years.

The vineyard, which also sells grapes to other Island wineries, grows a wide selection of vines. The major varieties are Pinot Gris, Auxerrois, Ortega and Pinot Noir; others include Madeleine Sylvaner, Muscat, Castel and Léon Millot. There is even a little Cabernet Sauvignon, Merlot and, until it was pulled out, Cabernet Franc. "My father-in-law liked the vines of his home region," Jim explains.

The Bordeaux varieties struggle to ripen on Vancouver Island but Vigneti Zanatta also finds the virtue in those grapes. The winery specializes in making sparkling wines, with four in its portfolio. The Island's cool vintages produce grapes that yield crisply fresh sparkling wine. "Low alcohol, high acid works great for me," Jim says. Cabernet Sauvignon, along with Castel, invariably goes into Taglio Rosso, a sparkling red. Pinot Noir is used in Allegria Brut Rosé while Pinot Gris is used for Fatima Brut.

The flagship sparkling wine is Glenora Fantasia, made since the first 1990 vintage and always made from British Columbia's only planting of Cayuga, a fruity New York hybrid. Cayuga was one of the most productive varieties in the Duncan Project. John Vielvoye, the provincial grape specialist overseeing the project, advised Dennis to plant it because it would be his "mortgage maker." Ironically, when the Vintners Quality Alliance rules were written by the British Columbia Wine Institute, Cayuga was not approved for VQA wines. Rather than stop making Glenora Fantasia from Cayuga, Vigneti Zanatta dropped out of the VQA program and the Wine Institute.

LORETTA ZANATTA

JIM MOODY

The winery's tasting room and its restaurant, Vinoteca on the Vineyard, is in a lovely restored 1903 farmhouse. Vinoteca, Vancouver Island's first winery restaurant, was opened in 1996 by Loretta's sister, Ileana. After her death the following year, family members added restaurant management to the rest of their duties. That often meant starting in the vineyard in the early morning and finishing up in the restaurant late at night. More recently, Vinoteca has been run under lease by local chefs.

MY PICKS

The Pinot Grigio, light and crisp in the Italian style that Dennis Zanatta loved, and the Damasco are tasting room favourites. The Pinot Nero (Italian for Pinot Noir) is light and refreshing. You should sample the sparkling wines over lunch. You will find the Glenora Fantasia shows the Cayuga's grapey flavours, Fatima Brut is rich and toasty, Allegria Brut Rosé has appealing hints of strawberry and Taglio Rosso has the satisfying fullness of a big red, but with bubbles.

SOUTHERN
GULF ISLANDS

GARRY OAKS WINERY

In 2008, winery owners Marcel Mercier and Elaine Kozak started to think of retiring and put Garry Oaks on the market. Taking their time to receive an acceptable offer (the winery was taken off the market in 2010) has delivered a bonus for fans of the Garry Oaks wines: more solid wines from this duo, one of the best teams in the wine industry. Marcel is a natural in the vineyard. "I've always had my fingers in the soil," he says, recounting that he grew prize-winning pumpkins as a child in his native Edmonton. Elaine turns his well-grown grapes into clean and complex wines, both in challenging years like 2007 and 2008 and great years like 2009.

This winery owns one of the best sites for growing grapes on the coast—a sunbathed slope overlooking the Burgoyne Valley, in a rain shadow on the south side of Mount Maxwell. It was carefully chosen when Marcel and Elaine left other careers in 1999—he was an environmental scientist and she was an economist. "I got all the soil maps and the climate maps and the topographical maps," Marcel says, recalling their property search. "This is kind of my systems approach." The qualities of this site stood out. Marcel, who did postgraduate work in land and environmental management, grins now when he relates that while he was at college, an aptitude test suggested he should really become a farmer. Instead, he had a career in international consulting until he tired of the travel.

When Elaine, the granddaughter of Ukrainian immigrants who homesteaded in Alberta, switched careers, her mother lamented, "What am I going to tell my friends?" Elaine prepared herself to make wine with an enology diploma from the University of Guelph as well as courses from the Wine & Spirit Education Trust. When she began making wine in 2003, she was mentored by Ross Mirko, an Okanagan winemaker, until he moved to New Zealand.

ELAINE KOZAK AND MARCEL MERCIER

The property, called Garry Oaks after the trees preserved on the hillside, once was part of a 32-hectare (80-acre) orchard. Since 2000, when they began planting, Marcel and Elaine have developed three hectares (7½ acres) with early-ripening varieties, including two clones of Pinot Noir, an Alsace clone of Gewürztraminer, Pinot Gris, Léon Millot and, with plants sourced from Austria, the island's first Zweigelt.

When the vines were young, Marcel and Elaine also made wine with Okanagan fruit, notably a Merlot that they called Fetish. Since at least 2008, Garry Oaks has made its wines exclusively with its own grapes. "We are seeing a consistent character presenting itself," Elaine says. "You see it more in our Pinot Gris. The fruit is brighter here [than in Okanagan wines]. There is a brightness and a cleanness and a minerality which is really complementary." And these flavours arrive at lower levels of alcohol than in the Okanagan.

"You always get the best expression of a fruit at the northernmost edge of its climate zone," Marcel asserts. "Here the Pinots, the Gewürztraminer and the

OPENED 2003

1880 Fulford-Ganges Road
Salt Spring Island, BC V8K 2A5
T 250.653.4687
W www.garryoakswine.com

WHEN TO VISIT
Open daily noon – 5 pm July and August; weekends only in spring and fall

CONTINUED NEXT PAGE...

GARRY OAKS WINERY

CONTINUED

Zweigelt are performing well, and this is definitely the northernmost edge of the zone."

MY PICKS

Everything. There is a laser-bright focus to the flavours and aromas of the Gewürztraminer and Pinot Gris. The Blanc de Noir rosé invariably is tangy and refreshing. The Pinot Noir can be light but always delivers good flavour. The big red here is Zweigelt, a wine with spicy black cherry flavours.

MISTAKEN IDENTITY VINEYARDS

The unusual name for this Salt Spring Island winery was suggested, as you might guess, by a marketing company after the partners failed to create a name on their own. The cheekiness of Mistaken Identity appealed to them. It manages to be whimsical without being frivolous. It was also inspired by comments from tasters who took the wine to be from somewhere else, not from one of the Gulf Islands.

The six owners are Nanaimo chartered accountant Dave Baker and his wife, Lenora; his brother Ian and Ian's wife, Wendy; and Nanoose Bay investment advisor Cliff Broetz and his wife, Barbara Steele. During a lunch with Dave in mid-2007, Cliff remarked that he would like to own a winery—only to discover that Dave and Ian, a keen amateur winemaker, had the same ambition. Six weeks later Dave learned a Salt Spring Island vineyard was for sale. Before the grapes were ripe that fall, the partners had acquired the vineyard, which is only a kilometre from Ganges. Ian and Wendy left their jobs on Vancouver Island to manage the vineyard, make the wines and run the tasting room.

OPENED 2009

164 Norton Road
Salt Spring Island, BC V8K 2P5

T   250.538.9463
    1.877.918.2763 (toll free)

W www.mistakenidentityvine
   yards.com

WHEN TO VISIT
Open daily noon – 5 pm July through early September; weekends and holidays in May and June; weekends only in September; check website for off-season hours

L TO R: IAN BAKER, CLIFF BROETZ, BARBARA STEELE AND LENORA, DAVE AND WENDY BAKER

CONTINUED NEXT PAGE...

MISTAKEN IDENTITY VINEYARDS

CONTINUED

The three-hectare (7½-acre) vineyard had been developed since 2001 by an individual who planned a winery before changing his mind. The 7,300 vines growing here in 88 tidy rows give Ian many winemaking options: the varieties include four reds, Zweigelt, Pinot Noir, Agria and Léon Millot, and seven whites, Madeleine Angevine, Madeleine Sylvaner, Siegerrebe, Ortega, Reichensteiner, Pinot Gris and Chardonnay. These have all become components of Mistaken Identity's estate blends, Abbondante Bianco and Abbondante Rosso—except for the Chardonnay, which goes into Charmela, an apple-based dessert wine.

The vineyard is being farmed organically, even though this adds to the production costs. For example, Mistaken Identity uses various natural soil supplements that are five to six times more costly than synthetic fertilizer. The ban on chemical weed control means that this job is done manually. "We will keep growing organically as long as we can," Ian vows.

The winery also pays a premium to buy organic grapes from the Okanagan. The varieties include Merlot because tasting room visitors invariably want a red that is bigger than the light, if charming, island reds. Gewürztraminer also comes from the Okanagan, made here because Ian developed such an affinity for it when he was making wine with other amateurs in Nanaimo. A former fish hatchery manager and then a landscaper, Ian started with wine kits before moving to fresh grapes and joining the Nanaimo Winemakers club. There, he became so adept with Gewürztraminer that he twice won gold for the varietal at national competitions. He has lost none of his touch with that grape.

His first professional vintage was 2008. The partners had acquired the Salt Spring vineyard in time to harvest the 2007 grapes but, since they did not have a licence, those grapes went into a freezer for a year and were blended into the 2008 wines. Both were challenging cool and wet

vintages. Ian met the problems head on, making quite acceptable wine. "If that is as bad as it ever gets, we can get through it," he said in 2010. Of course, he was luxuriating in the quality of his 2009 wines, from a year that was one of the warmest and driest vintages on the Islands in memory.

MY PICKS

Abbondante Bianco and Abbondante Rosso are interesting and ever-changing blends (depending on the vintage) from estate-grown grapes. Organic grapes from the Okanagan often are blended with estate-grown Pinot Noir to make the winery's charming rosé. Don't miss the Gewürztraminer when it is available—a special wine because of the winemaker's passion for the variety.

MORNING BAY VINEYARD & ESTATE WINERY

There is a perhaps unintended symmetry to the vineyards on either side of Plumper Sound—Morning Bay Vineyard on the west and Saturna Island Vineyards on the east. Each is visible from the other vineyard. In 2001, Keith Watt and Barb Reid, his partner, created the vineyard at Morning Bay after volunteering to help plant vines on Saturna Island. At one time, the two wineries shared the same Okanagan consultant and have had wines produced for them in the Okanagan. And in 2010, both wineries were for sale in what may be a comment on the challenge of attracting traffic to island wineries.

Morning Bay is worth the trip just for its beauty. The vineyard, carved from a formerly steep and wooded slope on Mount Menzies, displays its 2.8 hectares (seven acres) of vines along 20 terraces. Every September since the winery opened, this has been the venue for a day-long concert featuring leading British Columbia musicians. This concert, and others throughout the season, is part of Keith's effort to attract visitors to this handsome winery.

Keith, an agricultural journalist, bought a forested oceanview property on Pender Island in 1992 and spent the better part of a decade growing organic fruits and vegetables before settling on grape growing. "I come to agriculture with my eyes open," Keith says. Born in Winnipeg in 1951, he once worked for an impecunious Ontario farmer whose barn had burned. He helped the farmer salvage and straighten used nails for its reconstruction. As a broadcaster for the Canadian Broadcasting Corporation in Edmonton, Keith produced farm shows and won awards for his agricultural documentaries. He was a media instructor at North Vancouver's Capilano College until giving in to the demands of vineyard development. "I really inaugurated this project on my 50th birthday," he said once. He took some time to tour New Zealand wineries in 2002 before planting his vineyard and, with an architect, designing the winery.

BARB REID AND KEITH WATT

This is real cool-climate viticulture, producing notably aromatic wines that are refreshing and crisp due to their vibrant acidity and their moderate alcohol levels. The slope and the southern exposure of Morning Bay's vineyard captures heat during the growing season, but the nearby ocean ensures average temperatures during the long, moderate growing season. The varieties grown here are those judged suitable for this terroir: two clones of Pinot Noir, Pinot Gris, Gewürztraminer, Riesling, Schönburger and Maréchal Foch. The first estate-grown wines, produced in the 2006 vintage, include a Burgundian Pinot Noir, a crisp white blend called Estate Bianco and a dry rosé called Estate Chiaretto. The objective is that island grapes will supply at least half Morning Bay's needs. Since Pender Island is not a place for growing big reds, Morning Bay contracts Okanagan fruit for its powerful, barrel-aged red and for several whites.

OPENED 2005

6621 Harbour Hill Drive
North Pender Island, BC
V0N 2M1

T 250.629.8351

W www.morningbay.ca

WHEN TO VISIT
Open 10 am – 5 pm Wednesday
to Sunday in summer; noon –
5 pm Friday to Sunday in winter;
and by appointment

LICENSED PICNIC AREA

Morning Bay's winery was built with kiln-dried lumber produced from trees logged to make room for the vineyard. The two-level gravity-flow winery is set amid the towering forest with views of the vineyard. The large tasting room door rolls back, allowing visitors to sit outdoors on the patio. It is a design that aims to impress. "When people visit your winery and find that the building is serious, they approach your wines seriously," Keith reasons.

MY PICKS

Current range not tasted.

SALT SPRING VINEYARDS

In the mid-1980s, a group of amateur grape growers, including Devlin and Joanne McIntyre, founded the Fraser Valley Wine Growers Association. The McIntyres, then doctors in Abbotsford, had planted a hobby vineyard with about 70 vines in 1985. Another Fraser Valley grower who attended some association meetings was Claude Violet, who opened the Domaine de Chaberton Estate Winery in 1991. The McIntyres nursed their growing interest in wine growing until 2008, when they took over Salt Spring Vineyards from retiring founders Janice and Bill Harkley. "We had a lot of common interests and a lot of common goals," Joanne says. "A sustainable vineyard. Good wine. A beautiful property."

Devlin, who was born in Thunder Bay in 1950, grew up in Regina and got a medical degree from the University of Saskatchewan. Joanne was born in Halifax in 1954. After getting a degree in oceanography, she almost completed a doctorate in microbiology but never got around to defending her thesis because she went to Queen's University to become a doctor. She met Devlin, who was there to become a surgeon. They practised briefly in Saskatoon before moving to Abbotsford in 1984. He spent the next 24 years as a general and vascular surgeon while Joanne worked in general practice.

The Fraser Valley hobby vineyard was planted in 1985 to test what varieties would thrive in the coastal climate. Devlin succeeded with Siegerrebe, Madeleine Angevine, Madeleine Sylvaner, Ortega, Reichensteiner, and Schönburger. "We have been growing and making wine in an amateur way since that time," he says. As their interest in wines grew, the McIntyres began vacationing in wine country in Europe and the United States. They also found time to join various wine societies, including the Opimian Society. Devlin developed such a keen palate that he was the top Opimian wine taster in British Columbia three

JOANNE AND DEVLIN MCINTYRE

times. They purchased property on Salt Spring Island in 2002, as a base for sailing, another of their passions. Now, they moor several boats there and one in the Caribbean.

Salt Spring Vineyards, which produces about 2,500 cases per year, initially made wines both from island grapes and Okanagan fruit, developing a considerable following for an Okanagan-grown Merlot. Beginning with the 2009 vintage, the winery now relies on island-grown grapes. "People don't come to Salt Spring Island to taste Okanagan wine," Devlin reasons. The varieties in their own vineyard include Pinot Gris, Chardonnay and Pinot Noir. In some vintages, winemaker Paul Troop has turned the Pinot Noir into a classic red Burgundy. Increasingly, the Pinot Noir and the Chardonnay are dedicated to Karma, the winery's bottle-fermented sparkling wine. It is Devlin's ambition to elevate Karma into one of Canada's top sparkling wines.

The vineyard also has varieties for a big red—Maréchal Foch and Léon Millot, which are made into a soft and juicy red called Millotage (a name

OPENED 2003

151 Lee Road (at 1700 block Fulford-Ganges Road) Salt Spring Island, BC V8K 2A5

T 250.653.9463

W www.saltspringvineyards.com

WHEN TO VISIT
Open daily 11 am – 5 pm mid-June through early September; noon – 5 pm Friday to Sunday mid-May to mid-June and September and October; closed November and January through March; check website for December hours

ACCOMMODATION
Bed and breakfast

PICNIC AREA

CONTINUED NEXT PAGE...

SALT SPRING VINEYARDS

CONTINUED

created by Janice Harkley). And from the abundant local blackberries, the winery makes a port-style wine. "It is so popular," Devlin says. "We have to cut off sales around the first of July so we have some left over for people to buy as Christmas presents."

MY PICKS

Start with the two aromatic whites, Pinot Gris and Aromata, a complex blend. The Blattner White, which is likely to get a name of its own, has a lovely core of honeyed fruit. Blanc de Noir is a fine summertime rosé. Millotage is a satisfying red while the Pinot Noir is elegant. Karma is a crisp, dry sparkling wine.

SATURNA ISLAND FAMILY ESTATE WINERY

Wine lovers might well look back on August 2008 as the month when the Saturna Island winery's fortunes took a turn for the better. Throughout its first decade, this winery had been struggling to get results from its vineyard which, at 24 hectares (60 acres), is the single largest planting on the Gulf Islands. Yet it had been producing as little as 18 tonnes of grapes, because many vines failed to yield ripe fruit from what is one of the coolest vineyards on the coast. Plumper Sound to the west, while offering a picture-postcard setting, also provides cool nights. This is a beautiful but challenging vineyard.

In August 2008, Larry Page, the Vancouver securities lawyer who owns the winery, hired Danny Hattingh and Megan DeVillieres, young South African wine-school graduates (both born in 1984) who were beginning careers in Canada. Both have diplomas from the Cape Institution for Agricultural Training at Elsenburg, Megan having spent two years in law school before deciding that, like her partner, she preferred working with plants. Danny had also picked up practical experience from 2005 to 2007 at six South African wineries and at Domaine Drouhin in Oregon. He and Megan first came to Canada to visit his stepfather, a doctor in Dawson Creek. Charmed with Canada,

OPENED 1998

8 Quarry Road
Saturna Island, BC V0N 2Y0

T   250.539.5139 or 250.539.3521
    1.877.918.3388 (toll free)

W www.saturnavineyards.com

WHEN TO VISIT
Open daily 11 am – 4:30 pm May through mid-October

RESTAURANT
Bistro
Open daily 11 am – 3:30 pm May through mid-October

MEGAN DEVILLIERES AND DANNY HATTINGH

CONTINUED NEXT PAGE...

SATURNA ISLAND FAMILY ESTATE WINERY

CONTINUED

they returned promptly to explore wine regions in Nova Scotia, Ontario and British Columbia. Saturna Island was one of the first wineries to respond to their résumés.

They set immediately to rehabilitating the underperforming vineyard. "We had very inexperienced help here and the vineyards got totally out of control," Larry acknowledges. "We were on the road to oblivion with the way the vineyard was." But the South Africans turned it around. The 17 hectares (42 acres) of vineyard, which Megan managed, produced 34 tonnes in the 2009 vintage and 40 tonnes in 2010. "We don't want to go much higher than that," Danny says, "but we could not go on producing 18 tonnes a year from this farm."

The high quality of the 2009 vintage gave a lift to what Danny could do in the winery. He made a rare full-bodied red wine from the best Pinot Noir and a delicious rosé from Pinot Noir that was not optimally ripe. The vineyard's small Merlot block never gets ripe enough for a big red wine. Danny made a light rosé instead. And with some of the Chardonnay, he made the first sparkling wine ever produced here. He thinks it is an obvious winemaking choice for this vineyard, with the potential of making one of the coast's best sparkling wines.

This is a vineyard that was conceived almost casually. In the early 1990s, Larry Page and some partners acquired a large block of property on Saturna Island, selling the lots on the shoreline for housing. When he wondered what to do with the inland 31.5-hectare (78-acre) plateau, a French restaurateur in Vancouver convinced him to plant grapes.

The south-facing vineyards back against the soaring granite of Mount Warburton Pike (named for an eccentric English explorer who once owned land on Saturna). The first of four vineyards, planted in 1995, is Rebecca Vineyard, named for Larry's daughter. Robyn's Vineyard, named for Larry's wife, was planted in 1996. The final two blocks, planted

HOOMAN HAFT BARADARAN

between 1998 and 2000, are called Longfield Vineyard and Falconridge Vineyard. The largest plantings in these four are Pinot Noir, Pinot Gris and Chardonnay, with small blocks of Gewürztraminer and Muscat and a so-called experimental block of Cabernet Sauvignon and Syrah.

Saturna Island made wine with Okanagan grapes until 2003, when it began to rely on its own vineyards, only to discover how challenging the cool site is. "Very difficult," Danny learned. "We work with what we have and try to make the best product out of it." There is a footnote to this story. Seized again with wanderlust, Danny and Megan left Saturna Island after the 2010 vintage to travel in South America—having left the vineyard and the wines much better than they found them. They were replaced by Hooman Haft Baradaran, a German-born sommelier with a winemaking degree from a British university. Hooman previously spent two years at St. Hubertus Estate Winery in the Okanagan.

MY PICKS

The sparkling wine (90 percent Chardonnay, 10 percent Pinot Gris) is a promising debut for this style at this winery. The Pinot Gris table wine has appealing guava and peach flavours. The unoaked Chardonnay is light but refreshingly crisp. The Gewürztraminer is another peachy white, while the rosé is fresh and lively with aromas and flavours of strawberry.

VANCOUVER ISLAND NORTH

BEAUFORT VINEYARD & ESTATE WINERY

When it opened in 2008, Beaufort Vineyard was the first winery in the Comox Valley (there now are four). In the 2009 vintage, owners Susan and Jeff Vandermolen released from their vineyard the two first commercial grape wines grown in the valley: a Siegerrebe and a big red blend called Ça Beautage (a play on Meritage). It speaks to their ability that both wines won awards in international competitions. It also speaks to the potential of the Comox Valley.

Both are trained for business: Susan, born in Chemainus in 1958, is a chemical engineer, and Jeff, born in Burlington in 1959, is a business graduate. Their previous careers in the oil industry overseas allowed them to travel and, almost always, find themselves in some wine region. They picked grapes at a Loire château in 1991 and came away from that experience, and 25 years of home winemaking, determined to have their own vineyard. When not travelling wine regions, they might go sailing. They have even named one of their wines Panacea, after the boat they sailed across the Atlantic in 2002.

They have a taste for exotic locations. That explains the unusual guardian of their vineyard, a carved cedar Moai modelled on the immense human-like stone carvings on Easter Island. The winery owners were enraptured with Easter Island's culture during a trip there in 1999. They experienced serenity radiating from the statues and have sought to replicate this in their vineyard.

They left the fast-paced oil industry in 2005 for the serenity of the Comox Valley, choosing this farm with its view of the Beaufort Mountains after looking at one hundred properties. The 34-hectare (84-acre) farm is about 10 minutes north of Courtenay. After clearing trees (one of which became the Moai) from a slope of sand and gravel, they planted three hectares (7½ acres) of vines in 2007 and have room to expand that four times. They chose early-ripening variet-

SUSAN AND JEFF VANDERMOLEN

ies: Siegerrebe, Schönburger, Ortega, Pinot Gris, Maréchal Foch, Léon Millot and Cabernet Foch. They recognize that the growing season in the valley is a little shorter than it is further south of Vancouver Island.

They also buy grapes from the South Okanagan, varieties that would not ripen on Vancouver Island, such as the Bordeaux varietals, destined for Chimera, their Meritage blend. Susan, who makes the wine, also blends Okanagan and Island grapes. "There are purists who would not consider blending from different regions," Jeff says. "We are not purists in that respect. We say let's just make the best wine that we can from what we've got." Necessity drives blends on occasion, such as in 2008, when they had to make wine after buying an Island-grown Maréchal Foch that was barely ripe. After a month of trials, they hit on a blend of 70 percent Foch with two Okanagan varieties, Syrah (20 percent) and Merlot (10 percent). The easygoing quaffing wine— "the hardest wine we ever made," Susan says—was released with the cheeky label Foreplay. A customer planning a

OPENED 2008

5854 Pickering Road
Courtenay, BC V9J 1T4

T 250.338.1357

W www.beaufortwines.ca

WHEN TO VISIT
Open noon – 5 pm Fridays and Saturdays June through mid-August; 11 am – 4 pm selected Saturdays in October and December as announced on the winery website

PICNIC AREA

SUSAN AND JEFF WITH THE VINEYARD MOAI

CONTINUED NEXT PAGE...

BEAUFORT VINEYARD & ESTATE WINERY

CONTINUED

wedding ordered this wine plus a wild-fermented Madeleine Sylvaner that was labelled The Wild Child.

Beaufort produces about 2,000 cases a year. Susan still makes the wine in a room on the ground floor of their house. The wine shop is tiny, and open only on weekends, yet they manage to pack in thousands of visitors each year, some lingering in the picnic area with a glass or two of wine. A new winery is planned next to the nearby barrel cellar in the future. "There is lots of pressure for us to expand," Jeff said in 2010. "We run out of wine so fast. But we are predominantly a two-person show and we are already working 70 hours a week. We don't want to work any more hours."

MY PICKS

Everything, notably Carpe Diem (the sparkling brut), the Siegerrebe, the Pinot Gris, the Gewürztraminer and the blends—Panacea (white), Chimera (Bordeaux blend) and Ça Beautage (estate-grown big red). Black Solera is a fortified blackberry wine that stands in nicely wherever port is needed.

BLUE MOON ESTATE WINERY

Traditional wine growers in Europe pay attention to the moon, adjusting activities such as planting, harvesting and bottling to lunar cycles. It should not be a surprise that George Ehrler and Marla Limousin also are aware of lunar cycles. The winery, after all, is called Blue Moon and all the wines have celestial names. At every full moon, there is a special feast in Chef Kathy Jerrit's culinary studio adjacent to the tasting room.

All that is consistent with the ambiance of Nature's Way Farm, the property that includes the winery and the cooking studio. The farm, which emerged more than two decades ago from a peaty swamp, is a remarkable spiritual and organic oasis only five minutes from downtown Courtenay. George and Marla bought the farm in 2004 and continued growing blueberries, strawberries, various other berries and salad greens. The winery decision was made one Christmas, after they sent more than 1,000 cards to the farm's best customers and realized that was a ready-made client list for wines.

"He's always wanted to make wine," Marla says of her husband. "We thought fruit wine is an emerging market. It is something we had done before and, through trial and error, figured it was a pretty good thing."

Marla, who is an urban planner and landscape architect, was born in France and grew up in Ontario. She went to the Arctic in 1980 to work on development projects. That is where she met George, an engineer who was born in Edmonton in 1958. They formed their own conulting company in 1996. After they moved to CONTINUED NEXT PAGE...

OPENED 2009

4905 Darcy Road
Courtenay, BC V9J 1R5
T 250.338.9765
W www.bluemoonwinery.ca

WHEN TO VISIT
Open daily 1 pm – 5:30 pm June through September; noon – 4 pm weekends the rest of the year; and by appointment

FOOD SERVICE
Tria Culinary Studio

BLUE MOON ESTATE WINERY

CONTINUED

Salt Spring Island in 1999 (primarily for the schooling needs of their two sons), they continued to work with clients in the North.

They moved to Nature's Way Farm because it represented a desirable style of life for their family. "We wanted that lifestyle of growing our own food, and having our kids know where food came from," Marla says.

The winery was accelerated in 2007 when Marshwood Estate Winery on Quadra Island closed and sold its equipment. In one move, Blue Moon acquired a good selection of tanks and other professional wine-making tools, including equipment for carbonizing sparkling wines. George has not yet made a sparkling wine. He has proceeded carefully, perfecting various fruit table wines under the mentorship of Okanagan wine consultant Todd Moore. He has succeeded with wines made from apples, blueberries and blackberries and is developing wines with strawberries, raspberries, pears and saskatoon berries.

The challenge is tackling what George calls the "stigma" of fruit wines. Some consumers, he has found, are reluctant "because some-body in the family used to make fruit wine that was simply sweet or terrible and they got their first drunk with it." His cleanly made wines debunk that image. George makes intensely flavoured wines, relying only on each fruit's natural juice. "The only water I add is when I am mixing the yeast," George says. The wines are either dry or just moder-ately sweet. "I personally like the dry style," he adds. "We have a lot of people who come in, find our wine is not sweet, and seem to like that."

That style is also supported by Kathy, the cooking studio chef. "The drier wines are far more food friendly," she says. "I have made surpris-ing combinations with these. It is so difficult to pair sweeter wine with food." One of her more original pairings: curry and Midnight, one of the blackberry wines.

Soleil, made from organic apples, won the winery's first medal (bronze) in a national wine competition in 2010. Other delicious wines here include Dusk (blueberries), Midnight (blackberries), Dark Side (port-style blackberry wine) and Eclipse (fortified blackberry/ blueberry blend).

GEORGE EHRLER AND MARLA LIMOUSIN

CARBREA VINEYARD & WINERY

Stephen Bishop got a surprise when he opened Hornby Island's first winery in 2006: an archaic provincial law, the so-called "tied house" rule from the early 20th century, prevented him from selling Carbrea wine at his family's other Hornby business, the historic Sea Breeze Lodge. Four years later, he admitted that he had yet to "make a dime" from the winery. His persistent lobbying of the government, however, may soon bear fruit with indications that the tied house rule will be eased at long last.

The rule prohibits any manufacturer of alcoholic beverages from selling them in any retail outlet owned by the same manufacturer. The rule was meant to stop brewers from buying hotels and bars to create a distribution chain that excluded competitors' beers. An exception was made for restaurants located at wineries when those licences were created in 1995. However, Sea Breeze Lodge is about four kilometres from Carbrea Winery.

Stephen was incredulous. "In this era of sustainable farming, agritourism, carbon footprints and shopping locally, it is unthinkable that my family business cannot list our wine," he argued in one of his many letters to politicians. Finally, the government seems to have accepted that liquor manufacturers are actually not interested in owning chains of restaurants, bars or hotels. Legislative revisions promised in 2010 should open the door for wineries to list their products in associated businesses. Currently, Carbrea is the only winery with an off-site restaurant.

Stephen, who was born in Edmonton in 1964, came to Hornby Island in 1972, when his parents bought Sea Breeze Lodge, a resort with 15 cottages and, of course, a restaurant. After running a mineral exploration company—Stephen is trained in business and mineral technology—he and his wife, Susan, began managing the Lodge in the early 1990s. Buying wine for the restaurant sparked Stephen's wine interest.

STEPHEN BISHOP

When a guest suggested that Hornby Island should have a vineyard, he agreed that it was a good idea.

In 2002 he planted about 1.8 hectares (four acres) of vines—about 4,000 plants—on a sunny property that he and Susan had acquired earlier as a site for a home away from the Lodge. He chose varieties that seemed to be thriving elsewhere in various island vineyards: Pinot Noir, Pinot Gris, Gewürztraminer and Agria. "I didn't want to be too much of a guinea pig," he says. Only the Gewürztraminer struggles to ripen. When he expands the vineyard—he has space to almost double it—he is considering planting some Blattner hybrids.

Because of the youth of his vines, Stephen, under the winemaking mentorship of Saanich vintner Ken Winchester, also makes Merlot and Chardonnay with Okanagan grapes. That makes for some intriguing dichotomies of style, since the Okanagan grapes are generally much riper than island grapes. In a recent vintage, a Carbrea Chardonnay, rich and fruity, had a generous 15 percent alcohol.

OPENED 2006

1885 Central Road
Hornby Island, BC V0R 1Z0

T 250.335.1240

W www.carbreavineyard.com

WHEN TO VISIT
Open noon – 6 pm Wednesday to Sunday in summer; 1 pm – 5 pm Saturday and Sunday in spring and fall; by appointment in winter

PICNIC FACILITIES

ACCOMMODATION
One-bedroom vineyard cottage

CONTINUED NEXT PAGE...

CARBREA VINEYARD & WINERY

Perhaps his best achievement as a winemaker is taming Agria, a gamey Hungarian red that has blood-red flesh as well as dark red tannin-laden skins. Other wineries have found that when Agria is fermented on the skins, the outcome can be a rustic monster. Stephen has always treated Agria like a white, pressing the juice off the skins before fermenting it. He makes a soft red with plum and cherry notes.

He even blends about 20 percent Agria into his wild blackberry wine, which is drier than most such wines. "It has almost a wine finish instead of a flabby fruit finish," he explains.

MY PICKS

The estate-grown Gewürztraminer shows delicate rose-petal aromas and fruit flavours in a good vintage. The Pinot Gris is crisp, with citrus flavours. The Pinot Noir's good colour and raspberry flavours are appealing. The Agria goes well with burgers.

CHASE & WARREN ESTATE WINERY

That winery owner Vaughan Chase is interested in birds is obvious from Chase & Warren's wine labels: most reproduce paintings of birds by an Alberni Valley artist. One of the wines, a red blend, has the image of a nesting hummingbird, inspired when the bird took up residence among the winery's farm equipment. Vaughan later salvaged the nest, an incredibly delicate structure made with spider webs, to display it in the tasting room. That is one of several reasons for visiting Port Alberni's first winery, arriving after a short drive from the town centre or by the Alberni Pacific Railway, the vintage steam train that stops at the top of the vineyard every Friday in summer.

Vaughan, who retired from a 30-year teaching career in 2010, was born in Victoria in 1950 but has lived in Port Alberni most of his life. That accounts for his decision to grow grapes in one of Vancouver Island's most challenging vineyard terroirs. While there are dry, hot summers to ripen grapes, torrential winter rains leach nutrients from the soil, which, being wet, warms slowly and prevents the vines from getting an

OPENED 2003

6253 Drinkwater Road
Port Alberni, BC V9Y 8W6
T 250.723.9463
W www.chaseandwarren.ca

WHEN TO VISIT
Open daily noon – 6 pm in summer and by appointment

VAUGHAN CHASE

CONTINUED NEXT PAGE...

CHASE & WARREN ESTATE WINERY

CONTINUED

early start in spring. To avoid leaving the roots in too much moisture, Vaughan has extensive drainage on his 3.2 hectares (eight acres), where plantings are being expanded to provide eventual self-sufficiency for the winery.

Vaughan and Joanne, his wife (who is also a teacher), have lived for years in a comfortable house at the top of a slope that they logged. Sometime in the early 1990s, home winemaker Ron Crema, who later helped Vaughan launch the winery before moving to Campbell River, told Vaughan that the "slope would really look nice with grapes on it." Vaughan was encouraged after planting a few Gewürztraminer vines and making wine successfully. He began reading books on wine growing, including a number brought back from a softball holiday in New Zealand (he used to play third base in an international league).

Vaughan consulted various experts, including the late John Harper, who fired his imagination with anecdotes about grape growing. "A grand old man," Vaughan remembers. "If it hadn't been for him, I don't think we'd be where we are."

Vineyard planting started in 1996. Vaughan got vines from several sources—Chardonnay cuttings from an Okanagan grower, Pinot Noir from John Harper, Bacchus cuttings from Claude Violet at Domaine de Chaberton and plants from a vine repository on the Saanich Peninsula. "There are 38 different varieties here," Vaughan says. Most are small plantings being tested for varieties that are most suitable. The most numerous varieties include Gewürztraminer, Bacchus, Muscat, Chardonnay and an interplanted plot of Pinot Gris and Auxerrois. These two varieties are picked and fermented together, producing a white blend that Vaughan calls Alsatia.

"The original idea was that I would focus on the German varieties, Pinot Gris and Gewürztraminer, because they would suit the seafood that we have in the area," Vaughan says. Several white blends are based on such aromatic Germanic varietals as Siegerrebe, Bacchus, and Oraniensteiner that he also has planted. He has considered making sparkling wine and he intends to increase the red varieties he grows. Until now, the winery has depended primarily on Okanagan grapes for its reds.

Sixty percent of Chase & Warren's wines are sold from the winery, a converted barn that Vaughan describes as "rustic." It annoys him at times that potential visitors "just circle the wagons and leave because it does not conform to their idea of a winery."

MY PICKS

Alsatia, a blend of Pinot Gris and Auxerrois, captures the house style of the white wines here— fruity and usually off-dry.

CHATEAU BEAUFORT NOBLE WINES & CORLAN VINEYARDS

Denman Island's agricultural history goes back 120 years. However, the island's viticulture began only in 2006, with coincidental purchases of vineyard sites by the owners of Chateau Beaufort and Corlan. As this book was being completed, yet a third Denman Island vineyard was under consideration. The only Gulf Island currently with three wineries is Salt Spring, which has 10 times Denman's population of about 1,200.

The principals at Chateau Beaufort are Max Campill de Wedges and his partner, Linda Elgert. The vineyard is not named for the Beaufort Mountains (which can be seen off to the west on Vancouver Island) but for former European chateaux from Max's convoluted genealogy. "Two old ladies of my ancestry, Blanche of Artois and Blanche of Lancaster, were the chatelaines of Beaufort in Champagne country," Max says. "I have 1,000 years of tradition."

Max was born in Portugal in 1949. He studied chemical engineering but, following family tradition, became an officer in the Portuguese navy. He left his native land in 1972 for Montreal, choosing Canada because a great-grandmother had been a cousin of Lord Stanley, this country's sixth Governor General. "That was a time when there was enormous political turmoil," he says of Portugal. "I could see the revolution coming. I left two years before the revolution." Settling in Vancouver two years later, he took up the career of claims adjuster with the provincial automobile insurer, putting aside his interest in wine, which is another family tradition.

"My great-grandfather had a very large estate and they did some very jolly, decent port wine," Max says. "I was raised as a kid dabbling with the wine. But I moved to Canada and the climate was not conducive to grapes. The idea of a vineyard was set aside until we came to the island."

In 2006 he and Linda, a former flight attendant, bought four hectares (10 acres) on the sunbathed west coast of Denman Island, bringing

MAX CAMPILL DE WEDGES

SELWYN AND PATRICIA JONES (PHOTO BY MAX CAMPILL DE WEDGES)

along four Maréchal Foch vines from their Vancouver balcony. That was the start of a vineyard planted since 2008 with Pinot Noir and Chardonnay, Max's preferred noble varieties, and several Blattner varieties.

"I set 1,000 cases as my limit," Max says of his winemaking plans. "I can produce 15 tons of good grapes here. That will give me 1,000 cases. I only want to produce the best. I will not compete with plonk."

Corlan Vineyard's owners, Patricia and Selwyn Jones, plan to make a similar volume from their 1.6-hectare (four-acre) planting, mainly of Maréchal Foch and Ortega. Their vineyard is on a south-facing slope not far from Chateau Beaufort. After clearing the forest from the slope, they planted in 2006, with about 5,000 vines that Selwyn propagated from cuttings in his own greenhouse.

Born in Wales in 1934, Selwyn spent a lifetime in plant propagation. After getting a diploma in horticulture, he began his career in Britain. The post-war government there was planting extensively, to build a lumber resource for a future war. When that policy was

CHATEAU BEAUFORT NOBLE WINES

OPENING PROPOSED FOR 2013

4796 Lacon Road, RR1
Denman Island, BC V0R 1T0
T 250.335.0019
W www.chateaubeaufort.ca

WHEN TO VISIT
To be established

CORLAN VINEYARDS

OPENING PROPOSED FOR 2012

8441 McFarlane Road
Denman Island, BC V0R 1T0
T 250.335.9132

WHEN TO VISIT
To be established

CONTINUED NEXT PAGE...

CHATEAU BEAUFORT NOBLE WINES & CORLAN VINEYARDS

CONTINUED

shelved, Selwyn resumed his career in British Columbia in 1967. At the time, the forest ministry was propagating millions of trees and giving them without charge to the forest companies for replanting. In 1980, when the government decided it should sell seedlings, Selwyn opened his own firm, Sylvan Vale Nursery, at Black Creek on Vancouver Island. Now run by his daughters, Iola and Siriol, Sylvan Vale has grown to 46 greenhouses for propagating seedlings.

Selwyn was introduced to viticulture when some of the new Cowichan Valley wineries asked him for grapevines in the early 1990s. He estimates that he propagated as many as 20,000 vines a year.

After retiring from the nursery, Selwyn and Pat operated a bed and breakfast near Courtenay. However, Pat, who grew up on Salt Spring Island, wanted to return to country living. They moved to a rural property on Denman Island and, because Selwyn does not want land to be idle, undertook the development of an organic vineyard. The first harvest is expected in 2011 and Pat, who has winemaking experience, will make the wines.

The vineyard name, Corlan, is Welsh for sheepfold, inspired by the sheep on this property. After raising big-framed Suffolk sheep for several years, Selwyn and Pat switched to Clun Forest (pronounced klin), a breed from Shropshire and Wales. The intent is to let the sheep graze on the grass between the vine rows and on the foliage. The small stature of the Clun sheep ensures they will strip the foliage only from the lower part of the vines, beneficially exposing the bunches to the sun.

COASTAL BLACK ESTATE WINERY

It seems that the Ludwig family never plunges into any activity in a small way. Former Merritt ranchers, Terry and Bonnie Ludwig, moved to Vancouver Island to start a farm from scratch. Within a few years they had purchased a property near Courtenay which, at its peak with 260 cows, was one of Vancouver Island's largest dairy farms, situated on 337 hectares (833 acres).

A few years ago, the Ludwigs called a family conference, recognizing that their family was developing diverse interests. One son, Philip, had a thriving sawmill, while a second son, Daniel, was moving into beekeeping. "We decided that no one wanted to get up at 3 am and milk on Christmas morning anymore," says winemaker Abel O'Brennan, who is married to Amanda, Terry and Bonnie's daughter.

The Ludwig family started changing directions in 2005, planting what has now become the largest blackberry farm in Canada, at 32 hectares (80 acres)—with so many vines of cultivated blackberries that a mechanical harvester is needed to pick the fruit. For good measure, they planted

OPENED 2010

2186 B Endall Road
Black Creek, BC V9J 1G8

T   250.337.8325

W www.coastalblack.ca

WHEN TO VISIT
Open 1 pm – 5:30 pm Thursday
to Saturday; 2 pm – 5:00 pm
Sunday

ABEL O'BRENNAN (PHOTO BY AMANDA O'BRENNAN)

CONTINUED NEXT PAGE...

raspberries and blueberries as well. Since the berries need to be pollinated, Daniel took over a local beekeeping business, expanding it to nearly 500 hives—half the ultimate target!

With the sale of the last dairy cows in 2009, the Ludwigs converted one of the farm's massive barns into a fruit winery, complete with an attractive tasting room. "We realized it was impossible to balance the dairy with a winery," Abel says and laughs. "People don't like to come to a winery and smell silage and cow poop." As usual, the winery is done on a large scale, equipped with enough stainless-steel tanks and barrels for 36,000 litres (4,000 cases) of wine. Fruit wines are ready to drink earlier than grape wines. "We could do 75,000 litres a year with the equipment we have now," Abel says. "Even if we do that, it only uses up about 25 percent of the fruit we are capable of growing here." The winery, while selling in the domestic market, also plans to develop export markets for its wines.

Even before the winery opened in the summer of 2010, the Ludwigs had already applied for a distilling licence (the big challenge was convincing the Agricultural Land Commission that this is appropriate on farmland). The object here is to distill from the farm's fruit the spirit needed to fortify Coastal Black's port-style dessert wines. Abel would also like to produce *eau de vie* products. "It will be a small run," he says. That is not the characteristic Ludwig scale, only because taxes on distilled products are extremely high. "It is basically impossible to make money at it now in this province," Abel laments.

Unlike the Ludwigs, Abel grew up on Vancouver Island. Born in Campbell River in 1984, the son of a logger, he has been off the Island to work (including in the Alberta oil patch) and to travel (in the tropics). His range of interests runs from falconry to horticulture; he was one of the proponents of the decision to plant blackberries, using New

Zealand–developed vines from nurseries in Oregon. It may seem odd to plant blackberries when wild Himalayan blackberries—the ones with nasty thorns—proliferate in every ditch on Vancouver Island. "These are much larger berries, higher in sugar and with no thorns," Abel explains.

To equip himself as a winemaker, Abel has given himself a basis with wine appreciation courses and arranged to mentor with Daniel Cosman, a Vancouver Island winemaker and vineyard consultant. "I had a basic knowledge of fermentation and I have been able to walk through it," Abel says. "That being said, fruit wines are easier to make." A confident young winemaker, he also made 6,000 litres (1,319 gallons) of mead with some of his brother-in-law's honey.

Coastal Black offers both dessert-style wines and table wines, including a barrel-aged fortified blackberry wine. Abel also makes a carbonated blackberry wine, having discovered it was popular in consumer tastings before the winery opened. And Abel is ready for the snobs who argue that fruit wines, not being made from grapes, should be called "alcohol fruit beverage." He stands up for fruit wines. "I am Irish by descent, so I have a little fight in me."

MY PICKS

The raspberry table wine captures the berry's vivid aroma and flavour. The raspberry and blackberry dessert wines are full and satisfying. The meads have not been tasted yet.

EMERALD COAST VINEYARDS

As Evan McLellan began planting his 4.8-hectare (12-acre) vineyard, he chose Madeleine Angevine as a major variety because he and Angelika, his wife, were especially fond of Domaine de Chaberton's Madeleine Angevine.

"Claude Violet was very helpful," Evan says, referring to the founder of Domaine, the largest winery in the Fraser Valley. "I phoned and asked him what he would charge for cuttings. I wanted a truckload of Madeleine Angevine cuttings." Claude asked whether he planned to make wine or just to propagate plants for sale. Evan replied that he intended to make wine. Claude said he could have all the cuttings he wanted in exchange for one bottle of wine when the winery opened. Sadly, Claude died in 2008, the year before Emerald Coast opened. "It's a debt I still owe," Evan says. "I had great respect for that fellow."

Evan, who was born in 1955, and Angelika both come from families that have been in agriculture in the Alberni Valley for generations. "My mom grew up here in the valley," Evan says. "She used to deliver milk in a wagon with her dad." Evan also had livestock before switching to grapevines. "Plants just seemed a little quieter," he chuckles. For all the farming in his family, much of his career has been spent running his own company, West Van Isle Contracting, specializing in heavy marine construction (docks, floats and dredging), largely for the forest industry. When the forest industry began to struggle, Evan and his family decided to diversify with a winery. "People have been drinking wine for a while now," Evan says. "They are not about to quit."

He first planted Schönburger in 1999, getting the vines from an Okanagan nursery. At the time, Vaughan Chase had begun planting vines just a few miles down the valley three years earlier. Evan and Vaughan only learned of each other because they had begun to deal with the same vine supplier on the Saanich Peninsula. If not for that supplier,

ANGELIKA AND EVAN MCLELLAN

they would probably have heard of each other from the Cowichan Valley pioneer grower John Harper, who sold them both some vines. Evan's Pinot Noir is the Marienfelder clone that Harper recommended for short-season vineyards.

The other varieties grown in Evan's vineyard include Reichensteiner (on Claude Violet's recommendation), Siegerrebe, Pinot Gris, Gamay, Dornfelder and Maréchal Foch. "I like Maréchal Foch, even though it is a hybrid," Evan says.

OPENED 2009

2787 Alberni Highway
Port Alberni, BC V9Y 8R2
T 250.724.1500 or 250.724.2300
W www.emeraldcoast
   vineyards.ca

WHEN TO VISIT
Open noon – 5 pm Tuesday to Sunday, May through October; check website for off-season hours

That red first impressed him when he and Angelika, who have often gone wine touring in the Okanagan, tasted it at Quails' Gate in the early 1990s.

Because the Alberni Valley gets summer temperatures above 30°C (86°F), ripening usually is not a problem (although Gewürztraminer has proved hard to ripen, the McLellans found). The bigger challenge is keeping birds, deer, bear and raccoon from getting to the grapes first. Helped by his son, Adam, and consultants George Phiniotis and Ron Taylor, Evan makes Emerald Coast's wines, including a port-style blackberry made with wild berries that Evan picked with his granddaughter. They discovered they had not picked enough berries when the popular wine sold out first.

The winery and wine shop are strategically located beside the heavily travelled highway to Tofino and Ucluelet on the Pacific coast. "There's about a million and a half people a year go by here," Evan says. "And then they turn around and come back." While the winery was erected only in 2009, the design has an attractive heritage look. The McLellans sawed much of the wood themselves, recycling CONTINUED NEXT PAGE...

EMERALD COAST VINEYARDS

CONTINUED

timbers from marine floats no longer in use. The winery also preserves heritage in another way: Emerald Coast's rosé is called Lady Rose, after the steamer that served the Alberni Inlet for many years before being turned into a floating restaurant on the west coast.

MY PICKS

Lady Rose is a tasty rosé blended from red varieties and Madeleine Angevine. Another effective blend is a wine called Schon/Gris, an off-dry combination of Schönburger and Pinot Gris. The Pinot Noir is light. The Gamay has attractive cherry and strawberry flavours.

40 KNOTS ESTATE WINERY

Occasionally, extra drama in this vineyard is provided by the thunder overhead of CF-18s, taking off or landing at the nearby Canadian Forces Base at Comox. Bill Montgomery and Michal, his wife, have grown accustomed to the roar of military aircraft since buying this property in 1990, but it still a thrill for visitors and for those tending the 32,000 vines here.

Growing wine is quite a departure from Bill's previous career. He grew up in Prince Rupert, where he was born in 1949. His father owned a towboat company there. Subsequently, Bill established his own towboat company, Burrard Towing, based in the Port of Vancouver. He and his wife moved to Comox after selling the company and for many years were hobby farmers with a few head of cattle. Bill delayed ordering grapevines for a number of years when, as he recalls, his wife said, "You can't do that—you have to be born into the industry." But most other new entrants into the wine business were hiring advisors and Bill decided to do the same.

He prepared the six-hectare (15-acre) vineyard on a gravel-rich plateau above the Powell River ferry dock, burying drain tiles so that the vines, supplied by a nursery in France, would not have so-called wet feet. The vines were planted in 2007 and 2008. About a quarter of the vineyard is in Pinot Noir. The other varieties include Chardonnay, Pinot Gris, Gamay and Merlot. The latter was

OPENING PROPOSED FOR 2011

2400 Anderton Road
Comox, BC V9M 4E5
T 250.941.8810
W www.40knotswinery.com

WHEN TO VISIT
To be established

BILL MONTGOMERY

CONTINUED NEXT PAGE...

40 KNOTS ESTATE WINERY

CONTINUED

a surprising choice for this cool growing region, a choice showing that advisors do not always get it right. Subsequently, Bill has begun converting that block to early ripening Siegerrebe.

The winemakers at 40 Knots, Natasha Ponich and consultant Christine Leroux, produced the first vintage, a few thousand litres, from a small harvest in 2009. "We made a very good Pinot Gris," Bill says. He expects to have wine for public sale in 2011 or 2012, depending how the vines produce fruit as they become established. "I am not rushing this," he says.

The winery and tasting room have been installed in a renovated former barn that overlooks the vines. The new structure is so grand that you would think Bill was, in fact, born into the wine business.

MY PICKS

Current range not tasted.

LITTLE TRIBUNE FARM & WINERY

The Vietnam War was escalating when Larry Pierce, then a young man in Texas, decided to seek conscientious-objector status from the local draft board. "I applied and I got it in about five days," he remembers. "I don't think they had ever seen one." That designation seems ironic, given his subsequent career as a combative lawyer in Vancouver and now as a colourful vintner on Hornby Island.

He was born in Missouri in 1947, the son of an engineer who instilled a taste for agriculture in Larry. "When I was a kid, we grew a garden in the back every year," Larry remembers. "We would grow something different each year. One year we grew these decorative gourds. Another time we grew cotton just to see what cotton looked like. And another time he got some peanut seeds." When Larry came to Canada in the late 1960s, after living a few years in San Francisco, he wanted to be a farmer.

His first farm was in Golden, British Columbia. The property was so high in the Rockies that it suffered killing August frosts, which ended that experiment with agriculture. He was not much luckier with cattle in New Brunswick. "I had about 25 head of beef cattle," he says. "I don't think there is a faster way to lose money." So he enrolled at the University of British Columbia's law school. Called to the bar in 1984, he specialized in personal injury litigation, becoming a self-described "thorn in the side of the disability insurance industry."

CONTINUED NEXT PAGE...

OPENING PROPOSED FOR 2011

6160 Central Road
Hornby Island, BC V0R 1Z0
T 250.335.2189

WHEN TO VISIT
To be established

LARRY PIERCE

LITTLE TRIBUNE FARM & WINERY

Twenty years of that was enough, however. "I just got sick of prac-tising law," he says. "I was swamped with work most of the time." So he decided to return to the land. In 2003, he and Margit, his partner, bought a farm near Hornby Island's Little Tribune Bay. They planted about a hectare of blueberries and such vegetables as corn and potatoes. And in 2008, they added 1.2 hectares (three acres) of organic grapes (Pinot Gris, Gewürztraminer and Sauvignon Blanc) and began develop-ing this winery. "I have always been a wine drinker," he says. "When I lived in San Francisco, I went to the Napa Valley and did wine tours when they were a new thing."

"I saw a marketing opportunity here," he says of his winery strategy. "I am a six-minute walk from the main beach down here. The winery will be visible from the road. It will be open all summer. I will have all the drop-in traffic that I can handle."

The winery, with the capacity to make about 1,200 cases a year, is an unusual design, with decorative, rammed-earth walls that make the building sturdy, energy efficient and eye catching. "It will be one of those must-see buildings on Hornby," Larry says, adding provocatively, "I hope it jump-starts this place."

That's the combative lawyer coming out again. In 2010 Larry orga-nized an online petition, rallying those Gulf Islanders who believe that the Islands Trust, which governs the islands, stifles development and needs a thorough review of its mandate.

MY PICKS
Range not tasted.

MIDDLE MOUNTAIN MEAD

Helen Grond's passion for mead began when her initial lavender planting proliferated to 2,000 plants on the hillside of this bucolic five-hectare (12-acre) property. While researching the uses of lavender and the other herbs she was growing, she came across metheglin, an herb-infused mead whose name is derived from the old Welsh word for medicine. It seemed that mead making would be a natural complement to the farm's herb production.

Helen, who has a master's degree in geology and expertise in platinum group metals, became an expert on mead's traditions. Honeymoon is said to refer to an old practice of getting a marriage off to a good start by giving newlyweds a month's supply of mead. History's oldest fermented beverage, it was integral to Norse and Celtic ceremony and occasionally gory myths. One involves a murdered god whose blood was mixed with mead to create the mead of inspiration, drops of which subsequently were scattered, inspiring poetry and insight from those on whom the drops fell. Middle Mountain has been making a Mead of Inspiration since 2008.

OPENED 2004

3505 Euston Road
Hornby Island, BC V0R 1Z0
T 250.335.1397
W www.middlemountainmead.com

WHEN TO VISIT
1 pm – 5 pm Wednesday to Sunday, July and August; 1 pm – 4 pm weekends, June and September; and by appointment

ACCOMMODATION
Ambrosia House and Cottage rentals

HELEN GROND

CONTINUED NEXT PAGE...

MIDDLE MOUNTAIN MEAD

CONTINUED

"I have always been more driven by the historical significance of mead than by anything else," she says. "Mead of Inspiration may be the most famous historical mead. All human creativity derived from this substance. There is no reality to it, but it was a legend that was passed on for eons." So she and partner Steve McGrath developed their own recipe. "Obviously, I am not using the blood of famous poets," she says with a laugh. "We did find it was a good opportunity to use a lot of very interesting things that grow here. What we ended up with is something that is wildly unique and exotic. It does not taste like any other wine that I have ever come across."

That explanation speaks to the arcane art of meads, which range from pure honey wines to complex blends, both dry and sweet. Middle Mountain's Green Tea Elixir includes ginger, teas and ginseng and is infused with nettles. That is a simple product compared to the Mead of Inspiration, which incorporates 10 berries in the blend along with numerous herbs and botanicals.

The farm, which Helen purchased in 1992, is now totally dedicated to the meadery. That includes as many beehives (about 10) as Hornby Island's limited berry production can support. Most of the honey is purchased from a beekeeper in northeastern British Columbia. The meads are produced essentially to organic standards, though they are not certified organic since it is impossible to assure that bees visit only organically grown plants. Middle Mountain makes about 5,000 to 6,000 litres (1,100 to 1,300 gallons) per year and has the capacity, though perhaps not the ambition, to double that output. "We have never really looked for customers," Helen says. "We are still just trying to meet the demand."

MY PICKS

Current range not tasted.

MILLSTONE ESTATE WINERY

A veteran realtor, Dale Shortt has driven all over Vancouver Island for his clients. The readings from his vehicle-mounted thermometer increased his confidence in the vineyard he planted in Nanaimo in 2005 in a valley beside the Millstone River. Temperatures there, he noted, were as warm as at many of the island's other vineyard sites. "I think Nanaimo is much better than Victoria, and it is probably comparable to some areas in Duncan," he says. "It is very warm where we are. It gets 100 above [degrees Fahrenheit] here."

He also drew confidence from Nanaimo's first commercial vineyard, which Millstone now farms. Dale had many conversations with the late Harry von Wolff, who planted on a property not far from Millstone in about 1990. Harry grew approximately two hectares (mostly Pinot Noir and Chardonnay) on a slope backing into a heat-absorbing cliff. The Chateau Wolff winery opened in 1998 and operated until Harry's death in 2005. Not interested in growing wine, his son, Michael, turned over management to Dale and a crew that includes a vineyard manager who grew

OPENED 2011

2300 East Wellington Road
Nanaimo. BC V9R 6V7

T 250.716.3549

W To be established.

WHEN TO VISIT
Call for hours

DALE SHORTT

CONTINUED NEXT PAGE...

MILLSTONE ESTATE WINERY

CONTINUED

up on a coffee plantation in Vietnam.

Dale brings a farming background to wine. He was born in 1953 and he grew up on a farm just outside the Saskatchewan town of Kerrobert—and he still owns land there. "My grandfather was a farmer, my dad was a farmer and I was a farmer," he says. Eventually, he moved into Saskatoon and into real estate sales, explaining that "We didn't make any money with wheat." His father retired to Vancouver Island and Dale, while visiting, found the climate appealing. He moved his real estate business to Nanaimo.

In 2000 he bought this 5.1-hectare (12.75-acre) forested riverside property just across East Wellington Road from city limits. "I still wanted to farm," he explains. "I logged it off. I thought, I don't want to put horses here; I will plant a vineyard. I have always thought about having a small vineyard and making wine, but I never thought of doing it commercially."

He planted 2.4 hectares (six acres) of vines, primarily Pinot Noir and Pinot Gris, with some Ortega, Maréchal Foch and Merlot. It was a learning experience: in the first year, deer grazed on the vines, setting him back by a year. There is now a deer fence around the property. Young vines need to be irrigated, but he was not allowed to tap the nearby river. So he built a spring-fed reservoir that holds 4.5 million litres (one million gallons) of water and installed efficient drip irrigation. The vines responded well, producing ripe, full-flavoured grapes in 2009. "I had really good sugar levels in 2009—better than in Duncan," he says.

Dale had never made wine before he planted grapes (although his father had been a keen home winemaker). To learn the art, he made port-style wine with the blackberries that grow wild along the river. The result has now become one of the wines featured in Millstone's tasting room.

He tried to hire a winemaker. When he found that consulting wine-makers in the Okanagan were going to consult primarily by telephone, he and Kristi, his daughter, took on the task. He has found mentorship on the island, notably Jim Moody of Vigneti Zanatta. "I just had to learn it," he says. "I think some of our wines are turning out pretty good." To prove the point, he draws a sample of an excellent 2009 Pinot Noir from one of the barrels in the winery.

The 232-square-metre (2,500-square-foot) winery is built primar-ily of cedar and hemlock that Dale logged on this site. Two storeys and capped with a red roof, the building accommodates winemaking and the wine shop on the ground floor, with space for hospitality events on the second. The wine shop gets what Dale calls a "vintage look" from its antique tasting bar, formerly a store counter from a Nanaimo building that dated from 1867.

MY PICKS

The Pinot Noir has classic cherry and raspberry flavours, and a full texture. The Pinot Gris displays the bright acidity typical of Island wines. The blackberry "port" is medium-bodied and, happily, not too sweet.

MOOBERRY WINERY

There was an obvious logic in adding a winery to Clarke and Nancy Gourlay's charming Morningstar Farm near Parksville, the home of their renowned Little Qualicum Cheeseworks. "We'd been selling cheese to several wineries for some years," Clarke says. Like farm tours and other special events, the fruit wines available here draw additional visitors. Retail sales rose by a quarter in the first year that the wines were available.

Clarke, who was born in Toronto in 1964, and Nancy left Canada soon after they finished college to do missionary and humanitarian work. Their nine years abroad included work in refugee camps in Turkey and Afghanistan and culminated in duty with a Swiss-based humanitarian group. There, the couple became interested in cheese. Returning to Canada in 1999 and a home in the Fraser Valley, they identified cheese making as a significant business opportunity. Nancy returned to Switzerland to pick the brains of the cheese makers there before the couple launched Little Qualicum Cheeseworks in 2001. After three years on leased property, they purchased 31-hectare (68-acre) Morningstar Farm in order to expand their cow herd (now about 60 head) as cheese sales rose. It is a point of pride that their well-treated cows were the first dairy head in British Columbia to be certified by the SPCA. Nancy, the cheese maker, currently produces about nine different cheeses, ranging from brie-style to a Swiss-style hard cheese named Rathtrevor, after the local park.

They recruited partners to launch the winery: Phil and Laura Charlebois. Born in Edmonton in 1963, Phil worked in the lumber industry until moving to Vancouver Island, eventually coming to work at Morningstar Farm. "Clarke needed help on his farm," Phil recounts. "He needed help for two weeks and that turned into full-time employment. Originally, it was just working with the cows and doing farm

PHIL CHARLEBOIS

work. Then I got involved in making cheese as well."

There was little in Phil's previous careers to do with wine but that did not deter him from agreeing enthusiastically to become Clarke's winemaking partner. "I had tried my hand at home wine-making," Phil says. To take him the next step, the partners brought in consulting winemaker Ron Taylor to mentor MooBerry through its initial vintages.

OPENED 2009

403 Lowry's Road
Parksville. BC V9P 2B5
T   250.954.3931
W www.mooberrywinery.com

WHEN TO VISIT
Open daily 9 am – 5 pm

The winery opened briefly as Morningstar Creek Winery until Morning Bay Vineyard and Estate Winery on Pender Island drew attention to its various trademarks around that name. "So we had a contest for a new name," Phil says. The competition, which offered a case of wine to the winner, attracted about 400 entries. The winery owners created a short list and then settled on MooBerry. It resonates with them and with visitors who also come to the farm to learn about cows. One day last year, one visitor approached Phil in the tasting room to ask why one cow's enlarged udder was oozing milk. "She's about to give birth," Phil explained, as happy to educate about cows as about fruit wines.

"Port is what got me interested in fruit wines," he says. "I love port." Phil now makes a dozen fruit wines, ranging from what is described as a "rustic dry" cherry wine to sparkling blackberry. "One of the benefits of being a fruit winery is that there is such a wide variety of flavours that there is something for everyone," he says. He admits that he was once a "die-hard Cabernet Sauvignon drinker. I can't believe what I was missing out on."

The bestsellers here are wines made from blackberries and gooseber-ries. The gooseberry wine has tangy and CONTINUED NEXT PAGE...

MOOBERRY WINERY

CONTINUED

smoky flavours and an appealing rose-coloured hue. "If I have a red-wine drinker, I will pour him the gooseberry," Phil says. "It has such unique flavours—tart fruit with citrus." It is balanced to finish dry. Phil produces both dry table wines (including cherry, apple and pear) and sweeter dessert wines. Some of the fruit, including blackberries, is grown on the farm.

MY PICKS

The apple wine reflects the zesty, refreshing flavours of Granny Smith apples. The subtle pear wine is fresh and crisp, while the dry cherry wine has almond flavours that come from leaving the pits in during fermentation. The cherry dessert wine has ripe berry flavours. The raspberry dessert wine is as tasty as a bowl full of berries. And the gooseberry is unique indeed.

SOUTHEND FARM VINEYARDS

The 2009 vintage is forever memorable to Ben McGuffie and Jill Ogasawara, the youthful owners of SouthEnd Farm Vineyards, because their daughter, Miwa, was born in the middle of the harvest. And that was not the only remarkable thing about the harvest. Ben picked the last of their Ortega on September 26, the day after Miwa's birth. Well, not quite all of the Ortega. About 137 kilograms (300 pounds) of fruit remained on the vines, because it started to rain and the grapes appeared to be rotting. Then it dried up and Ben discovered that the botrytis in his vineyard was not grey rot but noble rot. The grapes he picked on October 7 had concentrated the natural sugar almost to the level of icewine grapes.

"This has to be the rarest of rare wines," he says. "It is not often that you get a late harvest Ortega on the coast." The wine, which was packaged in half bottles, is named Miwa. Since botrytized wines age well, there could be a bottle or two waiting for her when she is old enough to enjoy it.

Ben and Jill are the youngest couple to start a winery on the British Columbia coast: he was born in 1977, she in 1976. Their capital came from the sale of the apartment in Vancouver they owned when they were at university and were beginning their careers there. "We decided that we did not like Vancouver all that much," Jill says.

They are island people, after all. Ben grew up on Quadra, the son of a commercial fisherman and millwright. Ben's great-uncle, George Rose, who managed the island's roads, is CONTINUED NEXT PAGE...

OPENED 2009

319 Sutil Road, Quathiaski Cove
Quadra Island, BC V0P 1N0
T   250.285.2257
W www.southend.ca

WHEN TO VISIT
Open 10 am – 5 pm Friday to
Monday, May through early
September; noon – 5 pm
Saturday, fall and winter; and
by appointment

SOUTHEND FARM VINEYARDS

CONTINUED

believed to have homesteaded this five-hectare (12½-acre) farm in the 1940s. When Ben's parents took over the farm, they built the log cabin that has now been converted to the winery's tasting room. A chemical engineer, he juggled the winery with a job at Campbell River's pulp mill until it closed in 2009. "I am still short on time," he says and laughs. "I don't know what I would have done if I was still working."

Jill was born in Vancouver and grew up in a logging community near Campbell River. After high school—where she and Ben met—she got a forestry degree and then qualified in landscape architecture. While she has never practised, her training has gone into the design of the vineyard and the buildings at SouthEnd Farm.

She has taken a major role in viticulture and winemaking, mentored by consulting winemaker Todd Moore. The winery's sparkling wine—named Jimmy K after an effervescent friend—won a silver medal in the first important competition that SouthEnd Farm entered. "I think that is the way to go with our grapes here," she says, referring to the Quadra Island season. "The Pinot Gris and the Pinot Noir especially don't ripen enough [for still wine]. But they come in with the perfect numbers for sparkling."

Since 2006, Ben and Jill have planted about 1.6 hectares (four acres) on the family farm, which they now own and on which the winery is located. The varieties include Siegerrebe, Maréchal Foch and Petite Milo, a Blattner white. They also buy the grapes from Nevermore Vineyards, the property that once supported Marshwood Estate Winery (Quadra Island's first winery, it opened in 2004 and closed in 2008 when the property changed hands). This vineyard supplies Ortega, Agria, Pinot Gris, Pinot Noir and Dornfelder.

Ben and Jill plan to produce between 1,000 and 1,500 cases of wine annually, selling most of it from their wine shop. The wine is made only from Quadra Island grapes. "If you want an Okanagan wine, go to the Okanagan," Ben says. "You don't buy a Burgundy in Bordeaux."

MY PICKS

The Ortega and the Siegerrebe are the flagship white wines. Black Crow is a tasty blend of red grapes. Jimmy K is a crisp sparkling wine. The remarkable Miwa is probably not available anymore, unfortunately.

BEN MCGUFFIE AND JILL OGASAWARA WITH BABY MIWA

FRASER VALLEY

BLACKWOOD LANE VINEYARDS & WINERY

Until recently, Blackwood Lane bought some of its Cabernet Sauvignon grapes from the U2 block at Inkameep Vineyards in the Okanagan. It is a rich coincidence that there is a legendary Irish rock band also called U2. A few years after U2 was formed in 1976, Charles Herrold, one of the founders of Blackwood Lane, also set out to be a rock musician, first in his native Iowa (where he was born in 1959) and then when he moved to Canada in 1981. "I was offered a gig with Bryan Adams when I first moved here and I didn't know who he was," he says ruefully. He never did play his bass guitar with the rising Canadian star's band. Charles left music in 1987 to start several businesses, after having acquired his taste for good wine during his years as a musician.

His winemaking career began inauspiciously in 1990 with a kit that he won at an Italian cultural festival. He was encouraged by a close friend who was a good home winemaker. Soon, he was making wine with California grapes and, since 1997, with Okanagan grapes. By 2004 he had teamed up with inventor and former restaurateur Carlos Lee to launch Blackwood Lane, which is named for the White Rock street were Charles lives. Carlos was born in Korea in 1961, the son of a diplomat, but grew up in Peru, which explains his Spanish given name. In early 2011, Charles, by then involved in winery projects in Washington State, sold his interest in Blackwood Lane to Carlos.

Blackwood Lane began selling its wines in 2007 to private customers and restaurants. It opened its winery and tasting room in 2009 on a bucolic south Langley farm with a view of Mount Baker. A serviceable barn was renovated and air conditioned for wine production. A sprawling hilltop bungalow was turned into a wine shop. Long-term plans call for tunnelling wine caves into the hillside, perhaps with tasting rooms. The plan was put on hold in 2010 when Carlos began negotiating to buy a vineyard, and possibly a new home for Blackwood Lane, near Osoyoos in the south Okanagan.

CARLOS LEE

CHARLES HERROLD

Almost all of Blackwood Lane's grapes already come from Oliver and Osoyoos vineyards that grow the ripe, full-flavoured fruit for the winery's signature style. Blackwood Lane wines, primarily Bordeaux reds, are invariably big and bold, and they are priced accordingly.

The flagship blends are The Refèrence and Alliànce. The former is a Merlot-driven blend also incorporating four other Bordeaux reds. The wine is aged about two years entirely in French oak, mostly 500-litre puncheons that impart very subtle oak and showcase the fruit flavours and the elegance. Alliànce is a blend of Cabernet Sauvignon, Merlot and Cabernet Franc, aged about two years in a combination of small French and American barrels, which add a vanilla note to the taste.

The current portfolio includes Merlot and Cabernet Franc, with Syrah, Viognier and a Merlot-based port wine coming in the future from Okanagan grapes.

OPENED 2007

25180 8th Avenue
Langley, BC V4W 2G8

T 604.856.5787

W www.blackwoodlanewinery.com

WHEN TO VISIT
Open 11 am – 5 pm Wednesday
to Sunday

MY PICKS

The Refèrence and Alliànce are powerful yet elegant red blends with a structure (and price) that aims them at the cellar of collectors. Cabernet Franc and Merlot are intense and concentrated wines. Vicuña Roja and Vicuña Blanco are affordable blends.

BLUE HERON FRUIT WINERY

At 84, George Flynn gave new meaning to the term "estate winery." As he was completing his wine shop at the end of 2003, he explained that "it adds value to the estate" to establish a winery on the cranberry and blueberry farm he has owned since 1946. Now one of two fruit wineries north of the Fraser River, it was inspired by the success of The Fort Wine Company across the river at Fort Langley.

After returning from service in Europe during World War II, George bought this eight-hectare (20-acre) rural property on Dewdney Trunk Road—then a rural area, now a rapidly developing suburb. George eventually planted blueberries but earned a living in marine construction, applying the engineering skills he had acquired in the army. He still reflects on the irony of building docks and bridges after having once blown them up on another continent. "A lot of loud noises," he remembers.

After retiring from construction in the mid-1980s, he expanded to the several cranberry bogs. "Up until the end of the 20th century, there was nothing but money from cranberries—until everybody in the country started planting them," George says. The collapse in cranberry prices (there has been a recovery) was the catalyst behind his decision to research and then build a fruit winery. This was, of course, the same impetus behind the development of The Fort winery, which opened in 2001. George arranged to have The Fort produce the initial wines for Blue Heron Fruit Winery (named for the abundant heron population in the area).

However, George found expertise within his family to develop the winery. One son, a union business manager, steered the winery application through the regulators. Another, an engineer, designed the building, a simple and efficient structure with cedar siding and a veranda on the front, not unlike the period architecture around Fort Langley.

A daughter, an accountant, helped set up the business systems. In 2006 George's son Richard, who had retired early from an engineering job, agreed to take over making Blue Heron's wines.

The production, around 1,000 cases a year, responds to demand. Flynn Farms, the parent of Blue Heron, operates a long-established farm market each season for its cranberries and blueberries and, after nearly 50 years of selling berries, has many repeat customers.

MY PICKS

Current range not tasted.

OPENED 2004

18539 Dewdney Trunk Road
Pitt Meadows, BC V3Y 2R9

T   604.465.5563

W www.blueheronwinery.ca

WHEN TO VISIT
Open daily 10 am – 6 pm; check
with winery for holiday hours

RICHARD FLYNN

CAMPBELL'S GOLD HONEY FARM & MEADERY

Mike and Judy Campbell started keeping bees in the early 1990s, when a fellow church member asked to move her one hive from her urban home to their Abbotsford farm. By 2004, when he retired after 36 years of teaching, Mike had taken a beekeeping course and owned a growing empire of hives. Beekeeping, he says, is "very good for the soul."

In their red country store, the Campbells offer an astonishing array of honey bee products. As if the selection of natural honeys and honey-combs were not enough, there are more than a dozen flavoured honeys (from jalapeño pepper to Grand Marnier) as well as soothing lotions, healing products, candles and an ever-changing number of meads.

Born in Vancouver in 1946 and raised on an Abbotsford dairy farm, Mike began making wine in university. He became interested in mead in the 1960s, purchasing honey from a friend who kept hives near Peace River. Mike followed a recipe from a 19th-century medical book (a doctor's tonic honey wine) and liked the result well enough to continue making mead.

Applying the discipline of lifelong learning, Mike has turned himself into one of the Fraser Valley's greatest experts on beekeeping. Campbell's Gold Honey Farm's schedule of well-attended events includes beekeeping courses as the owners now seek to pass on what they have learned.

Mike Campbell's bees (and those of other beekeepers) are essential to the valley's berry farms. Effective pollination of blueberries, for example, requires four hives for each acre of berries. "Each blueberry flower needs to be visited at least four times," Mike says. "And there are seven million flowers per acre." The nectar the bees gather from the blossoms becomes honey, spawning the cornucopia of products in this store.

MY PICKS

Fruit-flavoured mead is called melomel. This winery has a wide range and I particularly like the wine-like Elderberry Melomel and the Raspberry Melomel.

OPENED 2008

2595 Lefeuvre Road
(280th Street)
Abbotsford, BC V4X 1L5

T 604.856.2125

W www.bchoney.com

WHEN TO VISIT
Open noon – 6 pm Tuesday to
Friday; 10 am – 5 pm Saturday;
noon – 5 pm Sunday; closed
Monday, all holidays, and
January

MIKE CAMPBELL

CONSTANTIN & VASILICA WINERY

This was British Columbia's first modern-era fruit winery when it was established in 1998 by John Stuyt, a Dutch-born horticulturist, who ran it for six years before becoming ill with cancer. One of his legacies is a hazelnut liqueur, still one of the tastiest products here.

John did not have a winery in mind when he bought the farm in 1989. He just believed that the Columbia Valley, which he found during a Sunday afternoon drive to Cultus Lake, is a superior place for growing berries and nuts. He planted hazelnut trees on half the property. On the rest he planted raspberries, blueberries, currants, gooseberries, saskatoon berries and eventually a modest vineyard. After making jams, jellies and other confections, he recruited winemaker Dominic Rivard, then just beginning to fashion his career as a maker of fruit wines.

In 2004, after John's death, his family sold this 16-hectare (40-acre) nut and berry farm at the south end of Cultus Lake to Constantin and Vasilica Nemtanu. They did not have a winery in mind either. After living a number of years in Montreal, they just wanted to bring up their family in the country. It was incidental that this quiet farm came with a winery and a vineyard.

The Nemtanus have a remarkable story about arriving in Canada in 1992. Both are from Romania. Vasilica was born in 1968 into a family of 16. She combined work and schooling to earn a university degree in agronomy before marrying. Constantin had been working in Holland, returned to Romania for a wife, and found Vasilica. In the turmoil surrounding the collapse of Romania's Communist government, they made their way to Belgium. There they arranged to stow away on a container before it was loaded onto a ship bound for Canada. They barely survived the 13-day voyage and were rescued after she banged on the container wall. "August 8, 1992," she says. "I will never forget. The police opened the container and gave us water and food. They

got a translator because I did not speak French, I only spoke Romanian." Within months, however, they had been cleared to remain in Canada. Over the next 12 years, they acquired and renovated a number of revenue houses before moving to British Columbia.

She had the training to manage the farm. For winemaking, she turned to consultant Ron Taylor. The former winemaker at Andrés Wines in Port Moody, Ron has become one the leading fruit wine consultants in British Columbia. "Thank God for Mr. Ron," says Vasilica, recognizing that she needed help to master the wine business.

The wine portfolio has changed little from the one originally created by Dominic. It includes a dry white currant wine made from a rarely grown variety called White Pearl, which John Stuyt sourced in Holland. One of the most popular wines is a blend of raspberry and redcurrant, called Velvet Royal. The fortified wines include a hazelnut liqueur, a unique product among the many produced by British Columbia's wineries.

OPENED 1998
(AS COLUMBIA VALLEY
CLASSICS WINERY)

1385 Frost Road
Lindell Beach, BC V2R 4X8
T 604.858.5222

WHEN TO VISIT
Open daily 10 am – 7 pm, April
through September; 10 am –
4 pm Wednesday to Sunday,
October through March

MY PICKS

The hazelnut liqueur is tasty, somewhat recalling an old sherry.

DOMAINE DE CHABERTON ESTATE WINERY

The largest block in this winery's 18-hectare (45-acre) Langley vine-yard is Bacchus, a floral, spicy variety that is perhaps the flagship white. Eugene Kwan, one of the owners, calls it his "100-mile wine," along with the Madeleine Angevine, Madeleine Sylvaner and Siegerrebe also grown here. The reference is to the 100-mile diet, the concept of conscientiously trying to eat and drink products produced within one hundred miles of where one lives, rather than from the other side of an increasingly stressed planet.

As it happens, most of British Columbia's wine consumers live less than one hundred miles from Domaine de Chaberton. Claude and Inge Violet, the founders of this winery, began planting vines here in 1982 because they wanted to be close to the future winery's customers. They migrated from France in 1979, where he had been a wine broker, and scouted numerous North American winery locations before becoming the Fraser Valley's pioneer wine growers. They planted white varieties, carefully chosen to mature well in the valley. When a demand emerged in the late 1990s for red wines, they backed growers in the South Okanagan, who still supply all of the winery's reds and the whites not grown in the valley.

When they decided to retire in 2005, they sold Domaine de Chaberton to Eugene, a Shanghai-born Vancouver lawyer, and a partner, Hong Kong businessman Anthony Cheng. A wine enthusiast with wine cellars in four cities around the world, he had been looking at wineries in Provence when Eugene introduced him to Domaine de Chaberton. Now, Anthony brings his refined palate to the blending of the premium wines here.

The winery had been named for a farm that Claude once had in France. The new owners kept the name, partly out of respect for Claude and Inge and partly because the brand is so well established in the Fraser Valley. They did, however, create the more contemporary label

EUGENE KWAN

Canoe Cove. "If I was 25 and saw a wine list," says Eugene, who was born in 1946, "I wouldn't order Domaine de Chaberton unless it was on the French side. I thought we should have something West Coast, New World."

The label obviously resonates with consumers. Since 2005, the winery has doubled production to around 45,000 cases a year. And Eugene has hung a handmade wooden canoe in the busy tasting room.

MY PICKS

More than 20 wines are offered under the two labels. Highlights among the excellent and reasonably priced Chaberton whites are Bacchus, Madeleine Sylvaner, Siegerrebe, Gewürztraminer, Pinot Gris and budget-priced Chaberton Blanc. The reds include Meritage, Syrah and Gamay Noir. Canoe Cove's highlights include North Bluff White, Chardonnay, Merlot, Cabernet Sauvignon and Shiraz.

OPENED 1991

1064 216 Street
Langley, BC V2Z 1R3

T   604.530.1736
    1.888.332.9463 (toll free)

W   www.domainedechaberton.com

WHEN TO VISIT
Open 10 am – 6 pm Monday to
Saturday; 11 am – 6 pm Sunday

RESTAURANT
Bacchus Bistro
Open 11:30 am – 3 pm
Wednesday to Sunday; 5:30 pm –
9:30 pm Friday and Saturday

RESERVATIONS RECOMMENDED
T   604.530.9694

THE FORT WINE COMPANY

A national historic park, Fort Langley still echoes the architecture and the daily life of the trading post established here by The Hudson's Bay Company in 1827. In 2002, when tugboat captain Wade Bauck built a winery on his cranberry bog only a short drive east of the park, both the design of the building and the name echoed the historic fort. Several years later, during a label redesign, he paid tribute to his own 35-year-long career by putting a tugboat on the label of Mighty Fraser, his red cranberry wine. If you don't find him at the winery, you'll know where he is.

Wade grew up in Ladner, the son of a tugboat captain, and became a tugboat deckhand after high school. After a few years crewing on tugs, he went to navigation school for the qualifications needed to become a captain. Since 1984 he has been a master with the Seaspan fleet of tugs, based primarily at the Roberts Bank Superport south of Vancouver.

"Tugboating allowed for a good deal of time off, so I thought I'd give cranberry farming a try," Wade said in a 2006 interview with *Mariner Life*, a trade journal. In 1988 he and George Flynn, one of his best friends, began looking for suitable property. George, who would later launch the Blue Heron Fruit Winery in Pitt Meadows, had retired from a marine construction company to grow blueberries and cranberries and talked Wade into farming as well. "Cranberries had always been the most profitable legal crop in North America," Wade told the trade journal. He farmed a small bog for a decade and had switched to the larger farm near Fort Langley when dropping cranberry prices triggered his decision to process some of the berries in a fruit winery. As it happens, the cranberry market eventually recovered and Wade gradually expanded his bog to 3.6 hectares (nine acres).

Currently, The Fort produces about a dozen wines. The portfolio has expanded and contracted over the years, reflecting what the

WADE BAUCK

various winemakers liked to make. The first winemaker was Dominic Rivard, a Quebec-born vintner with a penchant for dessert-style fruit wines. Then in the early part of his career, Dominic's talents took him to consulting assignments in Canada (he helped Alberta's fruit wineries get off the ground) and internationally, with projects in China and Thailand.

The team now in charge of The Fort's cellar is Toby Bowman, the resident winemaker, and Christine Leroux, the consulting winemaker. A Canadian with winemaking training from the University of Bordeaux, Christine has been a consultant in the Okanagan since 1998. Two of her other clients, Elephant Island Orchard Wines and Rustic Roots Winery, are also fruit wineries.

In 2008, when Wade noted that the winery's sales had plateaued, he decided to shake up the profile with new labels. Bernie Hadley-Beauregard, the Vancouver marketer who created the labels for Blasted Church and Dirty Laundry wineries, crafted labels that ranged from historical to whimsical and even provocative. The blueberry table

OPENED 2001

26151 84th Avenue
Langley, BC V1M 3M6

T 604.857.1101
  1.866.921.9463 (toll free)

W www.thefortwineco.com

WHEN TO VISIT
Open daily 11 am – 6 pm

RESTAURANT
Bistro
Open noon – 5 pm Friday to
Sunday

CONTINUED NEXT PAGE...

THE FORT WINE COMPANY

CONTINUED

wine, now called Valley Girl, has a label recalling a 1920s fruit packing box. The burly farmer on the label of Keremeos Fruit Stand, an apple and pear table wine, looks like a 1930s depiction of a Soviet farm hero. The raspberry dessert wine, called Finger Fruit, has a pretty blonde eating berries from the ends of her fingertips. The strawberry on Bite Me, the off-dry strawberry wine, is a sassy female with a provocative wink.

"We think it is fun and something that catches people's eyes," Wade says. "We are finding that older people can remember the nostalgia, and younger people appreciate the artwork. So it captures both those demographics."

MY PICKS

Mighty Fraser Red Cranberry pairs as nicely with turkey as cranberry sauce does. Ghost of the Bogs White Cranberry is a crisp, dry white aimed at seafood dishes. Keremeos Fruit Stand, slightly off-dry but well balanced, is recommended with pork. And Finger Fruit Raspberry is delicious on its own, or with chocolate or over ice cream.

KERMODE WILD BERRY WINES

Fritz Sprieszl has more imagination than the Liquor Control and Licensing Branch, the Victoria bureaucrats who regulate wineries. He and his brother, Bob, got a license in 2005 to make wines from—as the winery name suggests—wild berries. After the winery had been open a few years, the bureaucrats decided that, since it is a so-called "land-based" winery, it must grow some of its own fruit (as do all land-based wineries). Never mind that they had accepted the original business plan, in which Mother Nature grows the fruit all over British Columbia. What could Fritz do? He planted blueberries, strawberries and Fredonia grapes on this property, pacifying the regulators who seemed to have trouble with the wild berry concept.

OPENED 2006

8457 River Road South
Dewdney, BC V0M 1H0

T 604.814.3222

W www.kermodewildberry.com

WHEN TO VISIT
Open daily noon – 6 pm

FRITZ SPRIESZL

In fact, it is a great concept. The wines in the tasting room are unique. No one else has a wine quite as eccentric as the dry, smoky Sitka Mountain Ash wine or as ripe and delicious as the Blackcap Raspberry Port. There are about 40 edible berries in the wild, Fritz believes, and he is harnessing as many as possible to make some quite singular fruit wines. "When we walk into the forest, we see dollars," he says, smiling.

Born in 1967, Fritz worked in his father's Fraser Valley shingle mill until it closed. While his younger brother, Bob, went skiing in New Zealand and then farming in Japan, Fritz became a mushroom picker in northern British Columbia. That's when CONTINUED NEXT PAGE...

he began to notice the profusion of wild berries. He got the idea of making wine from a home winemaker on Haida Gwaii. After Fritz had refined his winemaking, he summoned Bob back from Japan to help launch the winery. Bob's wife, Kana, now often runs the tasting room. And the friendly winery dog is a rare Japanese hunting dog.

The winery's portfolio is approaching 20 wines, made from such berries as blueberry, salmonberry, salal berry, Oregon grape, elderberry, mountain cranberry, raspberry and saskatoon berry. Strawberry is coming soon, along with a semi-sweet wine made from Fredonia grapes, an old labrusca variety that he found growing in a nearby heritage vineyard. "I try to add at least two or three new wines every year," Fritz says. "There is so much fruit out there." Recent additions include apple wines (one crisp and dry, one off-dry) and new blends of fruit and grape wines, such as a Himalayan Blackberry/Merlot wine.

MY PICKS

The winery buys wild blackberries by the tonne (11 tonnes in one recent vintage), making delicious table and dessert wines. The off-dry Orange Salmonberry dessert wine is spicy and tangy. The Glacier Bear Dry Apple Wine is light, crisp and refreshing. And the Blackcap Raspberry Port, when available, is justifiably one of the most popular wines in the tasting room.

LOTUSLAND VINEYARDS

The lending library here is not advertised but if you are interested in nutrition and organic foods, you should ask what is available. David and Liz Avery have spent perhaps $1,000 on volumes that they are willing to lend. It is a personal commitment to spread the word on healthy living, part of this winery's green sensibility. The winery's machines run on biodiesel fuel. The wines are made from organic grapes and David is now taking that a step further by adopting biodynamic practices. David has spent much of the past decade planting other vineyards throughout the Fraser Valley with grape varieties that do not need to be sprayed with pesticides and herbicides.

Lotusland's owners came to wine through David's amateur winemaking and through Liz Avery's gardening. Born in Toronto in 1955, David was managing an office supply company until the winery and vineyard demanded his full-time attention. Liz was born in Paraguay, the daughter of a farmer who moved to Canada in 1973. The roadside property near Abbotsford was just a hayfield in a former gravel pit when the

OPENED 2002
(AS A'VERY FINE WINERY)

28450 King Road
Abbotsford, BC V4X 1B1
T 604.857.4188
W www.lotuslandvineyards.com

WHEN TO VISIT
Open 11 am – 6 pm Wednesday to Saturday and noon – 5 pm Sunday and Monday in summer; 11 am – 5 pm Thursday to Saturday and noon – 5 pm Sunday in winter

DAVID AVERY

CONTINUED NEXT PAGE...

LOTUSLAND VINEYARDS

CONTINUED

Averys bought it in 1996. They concluded that vines would thrive on the sandy soil, with its gently contoured south-facing slope.

Before ordering vines from an Ontario nursery in 1997, they sought advice from experienced growers in the Okanagan and nearby in the Fraser Valley. Claude Violet, the owner of Domaine de Chaberton, had been growing grapes near Langley since 1982. Most of Violet's vines are white varieties suited to the comparatively cool climate of the valley and to what consumers were drinking in the 1980s. But the trend had changed. "Plant red," Violet advised. Almost half the 2.6-hectare (6.5-acre) vineyard was planted to early-ripening clones of Pinot Noir, supplemented with several rows each of Pinot Meunier, Merlot, Cabernet Franc, Gamay and Zweigelt.

They launched the winery in 2002 as A'Very Fine Winery, a pun that was a little too clever. A year later they changed to Lotusland Vineyards. "Our old name was kind of cutesy, but it required too much explanation," David explains. He made the first commercial vintage in 2000, producing 2,800 litres (630 gallons). He made an enthusiastic jump to 54,000 litres (12,000 gallons) in 2001 (with the help of purchased grapes) before deciding that small is beautiful. Since 2003, he has limited his production to his own vineyard and fruit from nearby Fraser Valley growers.

After a few years of growing grapes, David revised his vineyard's variety dramatically. He replaced most of his original vines with the hybrid varieties developed by Swiss plant-breeder Valentin Blattner. These are low-maintenance vines designed to mature well in the Fraser Valley's climate. Since 2007, David has developed more than 40 hectares (100 acres) of vineyards for client growers in the Fraser Valley, planting Blattner vines almost exclusively. The Lotusland grapes, along with grapes from some of David's Fraser Valley clients, go into Lotusland wines, including a blend of Blattner reds. Unable to resist punning, David calls the wine "NV"—pronounced *envy*.

MY PICKS

The flagship white here is Girlsrmeaner, a Gewürztraminer blend produced both dry and off-dry. NV is a promising new red from the Blattner grapes. And if your taste runs to dry, fortified blackberry wine, try the Devil's Spit. The name alludes to a tale in English folklore in which the Devil lands in a thorny blackberry bush and curses it by spitting on it.

MT. LEHMAN WINERY

On a recent Saturday morning, the first two visitors to the Mt. Lehman wine shop seemed a bit unsure about what wine they liked. Vern Siemens, the owner and winemaker, immediately began to proselytize for his favourite. "If you are not drinking Pinot Noir, you should be," he advised. "It is all about silky mouthfeel. It goes with food. Pinot Noir is one of those wines that gets better with every sip, every glass." As you would expect, Pinot Noir comprises the largest block in his six hectares (15 acres) of vineyard and probably a large part of his cellar. "We drink Pinot Noir virtually every day," he says, speaking for himself and Charlene, his wife.

The view from Mt. Lehman's vineyards must surely be the envy of other Fraser Valley wineries. Perched on the hilltop, the vines undulate down southeastern slopes toward a valley dominated by snow-capped Mount Baker in the distance. It was this view that led Vern, a successful builder, and Charlene to build a home here and subsequently establish a winery.

Vern was born in Paraguay in 1956 but grew up in the Fraser Valley when his father, who had been involved in a Mennonite colony, moved the family to Canada. As a youth, Vern studied business and went on to be a land developer and builder. "That's why I can pay for my hobby," he says. "Construction pays the bills and I have a passion for wine."

"This has been my passion my whole life," he adds. "I was making wine in elementary school—dandelion wine. I have made wine from everything, from blackberries to dandelions to raspberries before moving on to bad grapes and then good grapes," he says. In 1991, a few years after he and Charlene moved onto this 32-hectare (80-acre) former dairy farm, he began experimenting with vines. Over the years, Vern estimates he has done trials with 50 or 60 varieties—everything from Dornfelder to Siegerrebe. Bottles of wine from these trials were often shared with friends, though Vern was disciplined enough to dump wines that did not please him. "This driveway is paved," he jokes "because we had to cover up all the red wine I poured on there in my learning years."

The successful varieties in the vineyard happen to coincide with the palate that he developed while collecting fine wines for his cellar. He has a special passion for Pinot Noir and now grows about half a dozen clones. He grows Pinot Gris, Chardonnay, Riesling and Ehrenfelser as well and is doing trials with some of Blattner's hybrids. His early conclusion from his winemaking trials is that the Cabernet Foch will have a useful future as a red blending wine and might make it as a single variety wine. He is less pleased with the aromas and flavours of the Cabernet Libre, seeing it as a blender at best. "On its own?" he says. "I don't think so."

He scaled up to make his first commercial vintage in 2008, using estate-grown grapes as well as Okanagan grapes. The winery is in the former dairy barn, with the tasting room adjacent to the nearby barrel cellar. Once he

OPENED 2009

5094 Mt. Lehman Road
Abbotsford, BC V4X 1Y3

T 604.746.2881
W www.mtlehmanwinery.ca

WHEN TO VISIT
Open 1 pm – 5 pm Thursday to
Sunday; and by appointment

VERN SIEMENS

CONTINUED NEXT PAGE...

MT. LEHMAN WINERY

CONTINUED

has established the brand, Vern plans to build a new winery to showcase both his wines and the stunning view.

The portfolio is extensive because Vern likes to make wine in small lots, including examples of big, rich Merlot and Cabernet Franc wines from Okanagan fruit. "Most of the lots I make are typically 150 to 200 cases," he says. "It is so much work doing it this way but it is fun. I get tired of drinking the same kind of wine. And I have these bigger wines just because some people, believe it or not, don't appreciate Pinot Noir."

MY PICKS

Forty years of winemaking and his acquaintance with fine wines have made Vern into an excellent winemaker. The impressive wines here include Pinot Noir, Pinot Gris, Chardonnay (especially the unoaked estate-grown Chardonnay), Cabernet Franc, Merlot and Cabernet Merlot. For an easy-drinking red, try Pioneer, a proprietary blend of eight red varieties.

NECK OF THE WOODS WINERY
& BACKYARD VINEYARDS

The name of this winery makes a point well worth repeating to the wine consumers of Metropolitan Vancouver, who are more likely to tour distant wine regions even though there is a burgeoning region in their "neck of the woods." In fact, the winery's owner, developer Ewen Stewart, operates two of the more than a dozen wineries in the neighbourhood. The other is Backyard Vineyards, under development near Abbotsford. It is so named because it is in Vancouver's backyard. The Backyard wines are available in the Neck of the Woods tasting room.

Gary Tayler, the winery's original owner, had called it Glenugie as a tribute to the heritage of his wife, Christina. Her family once had a farm in the valley, or glen, of the Ugie River in Scotland. Gary was born in Edmonton but is also of Scots heritage. Not surprisingly, the Glenugie tasting room and the wine labels featured tartans. He had been a grape grower in the Okanagan before becoming a builder in the Fraser Valley in 1988. A decade later, he planted a few Pinot Noir vines on his Langley farm. What began as a hobby vineyard swelled

OPENED 2002
(AS GLENUGIE WINERY)

3033 232nd Street
Langley, BC V2Z 3A8
T   604.539.9463
W www.neckofthewoods.ca

WHEN TO VISIT
Open daily 11 am – 6 pm

BACKYARD VINEYARDS

29418 Simpson Road
Abbotsford, BC V4X 0A6
W www.backyardwine.ca

WHEN TO VISIT
To be established

EWEN STEWART

CONTINUED NEXT PAGE...

NECK OF THE WOODS WINERY & BACKYARD VINEYARDS

CONTINUED

to two hectares (five acres). In turn, that led the Tayler family to build the substantial winery beside the vineyard, producing wines both from the estate vineyard and with purchased Okanagan grapes. A sparkling wine from the estate Pinot Noir was named Christina, another tribute from Gary to his wife.

But in 2008, after first Christina and then Gary died, the family sold the winery. Although the new owner is also of a Scots heritage, he has chosen to root the winery in the local neighbourhood. Born in Winnipeg in 1948, Ewen moved to British Columbia in 1981, pursuing a career as a real estate developer. He came into the wine business after taking over a struggling Abbotsford subdivision called Pepin Brook. Now the site of Backyard Vineyards, Pepin Brook included a vineyard and a commitment to build a winery. Ewen purchased the Tayler winery to harness its capacity for both wineries while building only a small winery at Pepin Brook until sales justify a larger one.

MY PICKS

The successor to Christina is Blanc de Noir Brut, a crisp sparkling wine made in the traditional Champagne method with Fraser Valley grapes. The winery's other Fraser Valley wines include Paradiso (a Zweigelt wine), a bigger Zweigelt under the Back Yard label, and a rosé blended with Zweigelt, Pinot Noir and Schönburger.

RIVER'S BEND WINERY

An especially appealing time to visit this winery is autumn, when the surrounding six hectares (15 acres) of vines hang heavy with ripening grapes. Delicious table grapes grow near the winery, more than the fresh market can absorb. With the winery's permission, you can sample grapes right from the vines and even pick your own.

A few years after buying this property in 1990, Court and Annette Faessler established the vineyard initially with table grapes. "We had a lot of grapes that we couldn't sell to the fresh market. So I started making wine myself and giving it away at Christmastime and stuff like that," he recalls. By the late 1990s, inspired by the rising number of Okanagan wineries, Court added wine grapes.

OPENED 2005

15560 Colebrook Road
Surrey, BC V3S 0L2

T   604.574.6106

W www.riversbendwinery.com

WHEN TO VISIT
Open daily 11 am – 6 pm
Tuesday to Sunday (to 5 pm in winter)

GARY FAESSLER

In 2005 the Faesslers opened what is the only winery in Surrey, naming it River's Bend because there is a bend in the nearby Serpentine River. Court's son Gary, who is a chef, food writer, and photographer, says he tried to talk his father out of opening a winery. But when his parent went ahead anyway, Gary became involved as sales manager.

Court was a vigorous senior when he launched the winery. Born in 1928, he grew up in the Cariboo, where his Swiss parents had a homestead. Court left school after the eighth grade and, after picking apples in the Okanagan, began working in construction in Vancouver. Strongly entrepreneurial, he soon had CONTINUED NEXT PAGE...

RIVER'S BEND WINERY

his own company, in 1952, the first of several that supplied wire rope and related supplies to contractors and logging companies. "I sold my company three times and started over," he said in a 2006 interview. By 2010, the winery was also for sale.

Winemaking for River's Bend began with the 2003 vintage, with consultants in the cellar. Starting with the 2007 vintage, winemaking has been done under the direction of Ron Taylor. Under Ron's hand, the winery makes big reds with Okanagan grapes. What he makes from the estate-grown grapes is entirely dependent on the Fraser Valley's variable climate. The winery's sparkling wine, Starry Night, takes good advantage of the high acidity in some vintages. Flaxen, the winery's flagship white wine, is a blend of several vintages, thus making a consistent wine by eliminating vintage peaks and valleys. In a tough vintage like 2010, virtually all of the red varieties in the vineyard were crushed for rosé. Ron has also made what he calls an "old time wine" with some of the labrusca table grapes.

The winery tasting room itself is a functional building with a shaded veranda along the two sides that looks over the vines. The winery has the capacity to produce between 2,000 and 3,000 cases per year.

MY PICKS

Flaxen is a tasty aromatic white with a core of sweet fruit. Blush tastes of strawberries, spice and candy. The big reds with Okanagan fruit are Black Horse—a blend based on Cabernet Sauvignon and Cabernet Franc—and Merlot/Cabernet.

ST. URBAN WINERY

This winery fulfills the passion that Paul Kompauer has had since childhood. "I am a seventh-generation winemaker from Slovakia," he says. "I made my first wine when I was 12, 13 years old, independently. And it was drinkable too." He was a 19-year-old university student in 1968 when Soviet tanks rolled into Czechoslovakia and accelerated his timetable to flee Marxism. "I didn't like the Communist regime and I always dreamed about the freedom of the west," Paul recalls.

He resumed studies at the University of Alberta, graduated in engineering, moved to milder British Columbia in 1976 and eventually set up his own consulting firm. Kathleen, his wife, who was born in Winnipeg, is also an engineering consultant (an authority on concrete technology). They delayed opening St. Urban for several years in part because their engineering practices have been so busy. "If it was up to me," Paul said wistfully in 2010, "I could sell the engineering business and retire here and the vineyard would be immaculate." And that was the other reason for delaying St. Urban: the three-hectare

OPENED 2010

47189 Bailey Road
Chilliwack, BC V2R 4S8

T 604.824.6233

W www.sturbanwinery.com

WHEN TO VISIT
Call to ensure the winery is open

PAUL KOMPAUER

CONTINUED NEXT PAGE...

ST. URBAN WINERY

(7½-acre) Chilliwack vineyard that they had purchased in 2001 needed significant renewal.

Paul grew up in the wine-growing village of Rača, a suburb of Bratislava, the capital of Slovakia. Once his engineering career was established in Canada, Paul picked up his wine-growing dream again in the 1980s by making an offer on a large vineyard in the Similkameen Valley. Unable to sell their Surrey home in a poor real estate market, Paul and Kathleen let the offer lapse.

A few years later, they found what was then known as the Back in Thyme Vineyard, just east of Chilliwack and four kilometres (2½ miles) south of the Trans-Canada Highway. The previous owner, Dennis Sept, had planted three hectares (7½ acres) of wine grapes, including Madeleine Angevine, Ortega, Kerner, Siegerrebe and Agria. His winery plans collapsed for personal reasons and the vineyard had been neglected for a couple of years by the time the Kompauers took over. Paul struggled to control the fungal diseases that had imbedded themselves among the vines. Finally, he pulled out all of the Madeleine Angevine and most of the Ortega, the varieties most often attacked by mould, and planted Gewürztraminer, Maréchal Foch and Zweigelt.

The Agria has also been pulled out, even though Paul likes the full-bodied oak-aged wines he made in 2002 and 2003. Not everyone likes the gamey flavours of Agria, he admits. His Foch-Zweigelt blend, to be released under a proprietary name, has taken its place as the big red at St. Urban.

Paul and Kathleen vacation on the Slovakian wine trail so regularly that, a few years ago, they bought a small house and vineyard across the street from Paul's birthplace. Members of his family tend the vines, making and selling modest quantities of white wine. In Chilliwack, they have recreated the ambiance of Slovakia. The tasting room décor, including the bright floral entrance, decorative glass in the windows and two statues of the saint after whom the winery is named, echoes Slovakia's cozy wine cellars.

"We were once visiting in this little town outside of Bratislava, called Pezinok," Paul remembers. "It's an old wine town with a museum of wine and grapes. We went there and found a big party in the little courtyard. They were celebrating St. Urban's Day." That inspired them to name their winery for the patron saint of vineyards. Many Slovakian wine towns have statues of the saint to protect the vines from frost. It is not entirely clear how an individual who was Pope for eight years in the third century achieved this distinction, but tradition has it that spring frost never occurs after May 25, St. Urban's Day.

MY PICKS

Try the Foch/Zweigelt blend. The winery is also releasing a Gewürztraminer and a white blend of Kerner and Siegerrebe.

TOWNSHIP 7 VINEYARDS & WINERY

Several Fraser Valley wineries, including Township 7, let you experience Okanagan wines without the long drive. Corey and Gwen Coleman, the original owners of this winery, believed they would be more successful at penetrating the Vancouver market if the wine shop was close to the city. Their second Township 7 winery evolved in 2004 from a Naramata Road vineyard development.

The Langley strategy worked. In 2006, when former restaurateur Mike Raffan bought both wineries, he discovered that 85 percent of Township 7's wine shop sales were at the Langley tasting room. Since then, Naramata Road has become of the Okanagan's most popular wine tour destinations and that wine shop now accounts for the majority of Township 7 sales. Even so, the Langley tasting room remains a favourite stop for Fraser Valley wine tourists.

The winery name is rooted in Langley history. The Colemans bought the property in 1999 and planted Pinot Noir, Chardonnay, Optima and a little Merlot in the 1.2 hectare (three-acre) vineyard near the 1929 farmhouse. (The Optima subsequently was replaced with more Pinot Noir.) When they read the legal description of the property, they discovered that this region was formerly called Township 7. The Colemans considered other winery names as well but Township 7 emerged, both for the history and because the Colemans considered seven their lucky number. The winery opened formally on the seventh day of the seventh month in 2001. The winery's sparkling wine is called Seven Stars.

The charming tasting room is housed in a 1950s farm building that is architecturally similar to the many riding stables in south Langley. While many of the wines available here are made in the Okanagan, the Township 7 wine shop retains the ambiance of the Langley countryside.

MY PICKS

The sparkling wine, made from the Langley vineyard, usually sells out quickly on release. The wine shop also sells excellent wines made at the Okanagan winery, including Chardonnay, Merlot, rosé and Syrah.

OPENED 2001

21152 16th Avenue
(at 212th Street)
Langley, BC V2Z 1K3
T 604.532.1766
W www.township7.com

WHEN TO VISIT
Open noon – 5 pm Thursday to
Sunday; noon – 4 pm Monday to
Wednesday

MIKE RAFFAN

VISTA D'ORO FARMS & WINERY

This is the story of how a creative winery has grown up from four mature walnut trees on this bucolic farm. In a career change from the corporate fast lane (both had worked with Ritchie Brothers Auctioneers), Patrick and Lee Murphy bought this four-hectare (10-acre) abandoned dairy farm in 1997. Their plan, after building a house, was to grow tomatoes, one of Patrick's passions, and to commercialize Lee's excellent fruit and vegetable preserves from their orchard. They now offer a remarkable selection—from heritage tomato plants to wines and foods—in a welcoming tasting room. "I want to have products where people go Wow!" Patrick says.

The four walnut trees were planted by an early owner of the farm. Patrick, who could have used the wood in the fine furniture he crafts, planned to make walnut oil until a friend, Jerome Dudicourt, gave him a family recipe for walnut wine from 18th-century France. The walnuts are picked in July as green fruit and macerated in brandy until the next spring. The walnuts (which by then look like soft black olives) are pressed and the liquid is blended primarily with Maréchal Foch and barrel-aged to produce D'oro. It became the winery's flagship product after Patrick extracted a licence from bureaucrats who were skeptical about walnut wine.

It helped Patrick's case with the regulators that he planted vines on the farm (Maréchal Foch, Ortega, Siegerrebe, Schönburger, Pinot Gris, Pinot Blanc and four rows of Grüner Veltliner) and contracted grapes from three Okanagan vineyards. Since the winery's first vintage in 2007, Patrick has built a portfolio that includes Syrah, Merlot, a red blend called Murphy's Law, and Pinot Noir, the Holy Grail for so many winemakers. "My philosophy as a winemaker is keeping the Pinot delicate," says Patrick, who gets the grapes from a cool vineyard in the North Okanagan. "I think it should be nice and light."

PATRICK MURPHY

Since Patrick and Lee farm organically, you just know that the walnut fruit is not discarded after being pressed for D'oro. The fruit is macerated a second time, 10 days in Pinot Noir, and pressed again to yield a sherry-style aperitif called Pinot Noix. Finally, the walnut fruit goes to Lee's kitchen to be turned into a tasty green walnut and grappa tapenade.

OPENED 2008

20856 4th Avenue
Langley, BC V2Z 1T6

T 604.514.3539

W www.vistadoro.com

WHEN TO VISIT
Open 10 am – 4 pm Thursday to
Saturday and by appointment

Patrick, who has taken winemaking courses in California and volunteered at co-operative wineries in France, also makes products from other farm fruit. There is plum brandy and a Somerset-style cider from the farm's apples. In the old French tradition, he makes Poire William, placing bottles over immature pears on the tree, ripening the pears in bottles over the summer and then filling each bottle with spirits. He might make only 30 to 60 bottles a year.

MY PICKS

I like the increasingly finessed Pinot Noir, the Merlot, the full-bodied Murphy's Law and the Syrah. The D'oro is original and tasty. The nutty Pinot Noix appeals to palates that appreciate dry sherry or single-malt Scotch.

VANCOUVER

ARTISAN SAKEMAKER AT GRANVILLE ISLAND

This is the tasting room for those who want beverages that are vegan and free of either sulphur or gluten. It is also for those who want to savour the taste of Masa Shiroki's authentic sake, including his truly original Champagne-style sake. And there are other surprises in this Granville Island boutique, including salad dressings, fruit juices and a remarkable ice cream, all incorporating sake rice. Visits to Canada's first sake house are an education in Japanese rice wine, from the rice plants growing in decorative planters around the small bistro patio to the production facilities visible just behind the tasting bar.

Now an evangelist for sake, Masa was born in Japan in 1950 into a family with "absolutely no connection" to sake production. He started his working career in the Tokyo office of the Bank of Montreal, which transferred him to Montreal in 1974 and then to Vancouver two years later. A few years later he became an air cargo executive in Vancouver with Japan Airlines; then he set up his own import-export company, dealing in Japanese goods. Eventually he ran the Japan desk for the British Columbia Trade Development Corporation. While helping Canadian companies sell microbrewery equipment in Japan, Masa met sake producers for the first time. In 2001 he began importing sake to British Columbia.

He soon absorbed the passion and the art of sake. "I have been blessed with my contacts in Japan," he says. "Every time I go back there"—he still imports sake even though he now makes it here—"I go right onto the floor of the sake wineries and acquire training."

Using polished rice imported from Japan, Masa bottled his first 600 bottles of sake just before Christmas in 2006. The products were so well received that by the end of that first year, he had produced 7,000 bottles. He now has a solid following in Vancouver restaurants, and not just for the sake. Many chefs use the sake lees (called *kasu*) because they are packed with flavour and nutrition. "The kasu has no sodium and absolutely no saturated fats," Masa says. "But look at the vitamins!"

The appeal of his Osake brand (which means "honourable sake") is its freshness. All of his products are unpasteurized or, as the labels say, *nama*. Each batch of sake yields several styles of beverage. Some might consider the cream of each batch to be the clear Osake Junmai Genshu, with about 17 percent alcohol. This sake is rich in texture, with fruity aromas but a dry finish. Masa pairs it with strong cheese or red meat. "Our message is that sake can go with cuisine other than Japanese," he says.

The equivalent of a white wine is achieved by adding water to reduce the alcohol a few degrees. This clear sake is Junmai, comparatively light and crisp. Masa pairs it with seafood. The third style, Junmai Nigori, is a deliberately cloudy beverage containing some of the rice lees, which contribute a creamy richness and a hint of sweetness. Masa also makes, in small volume, a more complex grade of sake called Ginjo, which calls for highly milled rice and

OPENED 2007

1339 Railspur Alley
Vancouver, BC V6H 4G9

T 604.685.7253

W www.osake.ca

WHEN TO VISIT
Open daily 11:30 am – 6 pm

MASA SHIROKI

CONTINUED NEXT PAGE...

ARTISAN SAKEMAKER AT GRANVILLE ISLAND

CONTINUED

special yeast. Made in both clear and cloudy versions, this grade is sold in half bottles. The bottle-fermented Champagne-style sake was developed more recently after Masa acquired a large following for carbonated sake.

Until recently, Masa has imported all his rice from Japan. In 2009, he began partnering with several farmers in southern British Columbia to find suitable sites for growing sake rice. "Our challenge is to convince the farmers that it can be possible to grow rice commercially," he says. His goal is virtual self-sufficiency with sake rice.

MY PICKS

Masa's sake wines are all sophisticated and tasty, pairing well not only with Japanese cuisine but also with a wide range of foods. Junmai is a good starter sake.

FORT BERENS ESTATE WINERY

Rolf de Bruin and Heleen Pannekoek, the Dutch immigrants who opened Lillooet's first winery in the fall of 2009, vacationed in Canada three times before settling here. The third vacation, in 2003, was spent in the Okanagan, researching a winery business plan.

Rolf, who was born in 1970, and Heleen, his wife, chose to leave high-powered careers in consulting and banking for the quiet lifestyle of small community winegrowers.

"One of the primary reasons why we chose to start a vineyard was that we could not foresee ourselves working in a corporate environment and having kids," says Rolf. (They now have two children.) "We are both very, very ambitious. We work incredibly hard to overcome our own shortcomings and excel. We knew that a vineyard and a winery will be a huge amount of work but we saw that as the opportunity to put our energy to good use. We find it very difficult to move at half pace."

By the time they got their immigrant visas in 2008, Okanagan vineyard land prices had soared, becoming dangerously out of reach for a new venture. But several of their Okanagan contacts suggested Lillooet, where grape-growing trials had been underway for several years. Rolf and Heleen sought advice from Christ'l Roshard, Lillooet's former mayor and an owner, with husband CONTINUED NEXT PAGE...

OPENED 2009

1881 Highway 99 North
Lillooet, BC V0K 1V0

T 250.256.7788
  1.877.956.7768 (toll free)

W www.fortberens.ca

WHEN TO VISIT
Open daily 10 am – 6 pm May through October; 10 am – 4 pm Wednesday to Sunday and holidays, November through April

ROLF DE BRUIN AND HELEEN PANNEKOEK

FORT BERENS ESTATE WINERY

Doug Robson, of a test vineyard. Then the Dutch couple spent the final four months of 2008 on a feasibility study before leasing (with an option to purchase) farmland strategically located beside a highway.

On land that once was a wartime tomato farm and then an experimental farm, they planted nine hectares (20 acres) of vines in 2009, devoting half of it to Pinot Noir and Riesling and completing the vineyard with Chardonnay, Pinot Gris, Merlot and Cabernet Franc. "The climate is very good in terms of growing degree days," Rolf says "It has some challenges regarding the length of the season, though the occurrence of frost in October and April is lower here than in Oliver." The first harvest from these vines is expected in 2011. By then Rolf and Heleen expect to have moved winemaking from a renovated tractor shed into a new 4,000-case winery. The new tasting room has a sweeping panorama of the mighty Fraser River and nearby mountains, which rise to 1,800 metres (6,000 feet).

The initial vintages, at least through 2010, are being made with Okanagan grapes from a Black Sage Road vineyard, with Rolf and Heleen working under the tutelage of veteran Okanagan grape growers and winemakers. "We actually have a team of consultants that we are working with," Rolf says. "We recognize that being new to the industry and starting a new region, there are a lot of risk factors."

The winery is named after the Hudson's Bay trading post that was started here in 1859 but never completed. "We chose Fort Berens because it leads into the history of this region," Rolf says.

MY PICKS

Of the debut wines, the standouts were Meritage, Cabernet Franc, Pinot Noir Rosé and Chardonnay.

ISABELLA WINERY

Isabella Winery is the exception to the rule that British Columbia wineries export few of their wines. Isabella exports about 60 percent of the 3.5 to 4 million bottles it produces each year, much of it marketed through five retail stores in China. Winery owner Tony Ouyang, who also operates a chain of nutrition stores in Vancouver, has the advantage of speaking Mandarin and knowing the Chinese business culture, having been born in Taiwan in 1965.

"Ever since I was a boy I dreamed of making wine," he says. Taiwan has a richer wine culture than is generally known. Many people make fruit wines at home. Since the government liberalized wine laws in 2002, more than one hundred wineries have been established. However, Tony had immigrated to North America before this burgeoning of wineries. After living in San Francisco, he moved to Vancouver in 1992 and established Capwork Nutrition.

Initially, Tony also tried to become a distributor of British Columbia wine in Asia and visited nearly every winery in the North Okanagan with this proposition. Vern Rose, the famously gregarious

OPENED 2007

11491 River Road
Richmond. BC V6X 1Z6

T 604.288.0608

W www.isabellawinery.com

WHEN TO VISIT
Open daily 11 am – 6 pm spring to fall; to 5 pm in late fall until seasonal closing November 15

TONY OUYANG

CONTINUED NEXT PAGE...

ISABELLA WINERY

CONTINUED

founder of the House of Rose winery in Rutland, invited Tony to stay at his home for a few days and regaled the would-be agent with wine talk. "When I heard his story and his history, his dream became my dream," Tony recalls.

When Tony set out to open his own winery, he was tempted to buy House of Rose. However, with children in school and a flourishing health-food business, moving to Kelowna was not an option. Instead Tony bought a former Richmond restaurant building on the banks of the Fraser River, developing his winery in an industrial and commercial area, with fish-packing plants as neighbours. The building was renovated to make its faux-castle appearance appealing for the growing number of wine tourists, especially from China, that stop here.

The winery is named after one of the earliest Spanish ships to sail into this area, since Tony has a fascination with all things Spanish. The Spanish allusion recalls that brief period in the early 17th century when the Spanish, from their base in the Philippines, established a fort and a colony on the north end of La Isla Hermosa, as they called Taiwan. The colony, meant to hold off Spain's rivals in the area (the Dutch and the Japanese), did not last long but still seems to resonate in Taiwan's history. Tony also maintains that a Latin version of his winery's name means "service to God." "What I have today, everything comes from God," he says.

Not having room for the vineyard or the orchard needed for a land-based winery, Tony opened Isabella under a commercial winery licence. This gives him the flexibility to import wine and grapes from the United States as well as source VQA wines from wineries in the Okanagan. Many of Isabella's icewines, for example, are produced for Tony by Kalala Organic Estate Winery in West Kelowna. Most of the VQA wines now are released under The Little Beaver label that Isabella

launched in 2010. The consulting winemaker is Charles Herrold, one of the founders of Langley's Blackwood Lane.

Tony's expertise is in making Isabella's fruit wines. "I have my own recipes," he says. His cranberry, raspberry, and blueberry dessert wines are remarkably full bodied, reflecting the high volume of natural juice that goes into making the wines. Some competing fruit wines are thin, he says provocatively, because water is cheaper than juice.

MY PICKS

The wines are all affordably priced. My favourites include The Little Beaver Attribute, a red blend based on the Bordeaux varieties, and The Little Beaver Viognier, a white with the classic honeysuckle and tropical fruit flavours of the variety. The rich flavours of the Isabella Blueberry dessert wine recall blueberry and blackcurrant jam. The Isabella Riesling Icewine is delicious.

LULU ISLAND WINERY

The grandest winery in the Fraser Delta is the 2,044 square-metre (22,000 square-foot) Lulu Island Winery that John Chang and Allison Lu opened in 2009. How grand is it? Well, during the 2010 Winter Olympics, the $3.5-million Spanish-style building backing onto 2.4 hectares (six acres) of vineyard was rented by China. It served as China House, a venue where the athletes could gather with Chinese media and officials for ceremonies, press conferences and meals.

John was born in Taiwan in 1955. Before coming to Canada he built a business as an electrical equipment dealer in Taiwan. As a young adult he took up the craft of making wines, having learned how to make fruit wines from Soo Gao Chang, his grandmother. He began to dream of having a winery of his own, not very practical in Taiwan, where the single winery at the time was state owned. But Canada provided him with the opportunity.

In Richmond, where they settled in 1999, John and Allison discovered flavoursome raspberries and blueberries, fruits not well known in Taiwan. John made a number of trial lots of fruit wines in small containers, then, with the help of a consulting winemaker, made commercial volumes in rented facilities in a Richmond strip mall. Late in 2001, they opened what they called Blossom Winery, then the only winery in Canada with Chinese owners. They closed Blossom when they moved to Lulu Island, keeping the name as a brand in export markets.

At Blossom, they focused initially on blueberry and raspberry wines, and also dabbled in cranberry and passion fruit wine. They even tried to develop a line of kosher wines but found the production requirements too onerous. Lulu Island still offers blueberry and raspberry wines but has a portfolio of grape wines, now the focus of wine production. In 2010, the winery substantially increased its portfolio to include at least eight grape table wines.

John was drawn into grape wines through icewine. Blossom began offering icewine not long after opening, John having spotted how popular it is in China and Taiwan. One of the few Mandarin speakers in the Canadian wine industry, John has represented Canadian icewines at many seminars in China. Lulu Island, which has grape contracts with about 10 vineyards in the Okanagan and the Similkameen Valley, keeps a press permanently in the Interior for the annual icewine harvests. It is impractical to truck the grapes to Richmond because they could thaw during the journey. By regulation, icewine grapes must be picked and crushed when they are frozen. Lulu Island's icewines are blends: the red is made with Merlot and Pinot Noir and the white with Riesling and Chardonnay.

OPENED 2009

16880 Westminster Highway
Richmond, BC V6V 1A8

T 604.232.9839

W www.luluislandwinery.com

WHEN TO VISIT
Open 10 am – 6:30 pm Monday
through Saturday

ALLISON LU AND JOHN CHANG

Lulu Island is a destination winery for inbound tours from Asia. The tasting-room employees are multilingual. With four tasting rooms, the winery can accommodate busloads of visitors in each of the three smaller tasting rooms and the general public in the large wine shop. "John wanted to set up the winery here because it is close to the airport," Allison explains. "People can taste Okanagan wine here without having to drive five hours to the Okanagan."

CONTINUED NEXT PAGE...

LULU ISLAND WINERY

CONTINUED

MY PICKS

The grape wines include an excellent Cabernet
Franc, along with easy-drinking Merlot, Shiraz
and Cabernet Sauvignon. The Bordeaux blend
formerly called Two Left Feet is now called
Meritage. The intensely tropical Sauvignon
Blanc is a crowd pleaser. The white icewine is
a fat, golden wine with flavours of citrus and
ripe pineapple while the red icewine tastes
of rose petals, plum jam and chocolate.

PACIFIC BREEZE WINERY

Pacific Breeze proudly calls itself a "garage winery" because its location in an industrial mall looks like former parking for a semi-trailer or two, and their tractors. There is a busy New Westminster truck route nearby and the SkyTrain line is almost overhead. But, in the best tradition of garage wineries, the wines in the compact tasting room are stunning.

Frank Gregus and Maurice Hamilton, the owners of this winery, are friends and long-time home winemakers who set out in 2005 to scout vineyards in California and Washington State for premium grapes. Their model was the garage wineries in Woodinville, a Seattle suburb, that craft great wines from carefully sourced grapes. None have vineyards of their own. Neither does Pacific Breeze: Frank and Maurice contract with growers committed to growing flavour-packed grapes on great sites.

OPENED 2007

6 – 320 Stewardson Way
New Westminster. BC V3M 6C3

T   604.522.2228

W   www.pacificbreezewinery.com

WHEN TO VISIT
Open noon – 5 pm Sunday to
Thursday; noon – 6 pm Friday
and Saturday

FRANK GREGUS AND MAURICE HAMILTON.
(PHOTO COURTESY OF PACIFIC BREEZE)

"It is important for us to work with the same vineyards," Frank says. "If we bounce around year after year, we will not get consistency." In Sonoma's Alexander Valley, for example, they found the aCURE eSTATE Vineyard (it is owned by two doctors) for one of Pacific Breeze's best Cabernet Sauvignons. In California's Lake County, they found premium sources of more Cabernet Sauvignon, other Bordeaux reds, and Syrah and other Rhone varietals. Chardonnay CONTINUED NEXT PAGE...

PACIFIC BREEZE WINERY

CONTINUED

comes from a top Carneros vineyard. These are crafted into powerful, premium-priced wines that, at $25 to $35 a bottle, still represent good value. Grapes from these same vineyards have ended up in $100 wines in California.

With refrigerated trucking, it is as easy to deliver those California grapes in prime condition as it would be if the grapes were from the Okanagan. When Frank and Maurice were launching Pacific Breeze, there was a shortage of Okanagan grapes. Eventually, they would like to use Okanagan grapes as well—perhaps even buy their own vineyard. "As amateurs, we made a lot of wine from BC grapes," Frank says.

Pacific Breeze now crafts about 5,000 cases of wine each year in its New Westminster garage, wines that deliver loads of flavour. The partners believe there is considerable potential to grow well beyond that volume, especially as the wine consumers of Greater Vancouver discover Pacific Breeze's funky little tasting room and wine shop, or find the wines in a growing number of restaurants.

MY PICKS

The Chardonnay shows the crisp, citrusy fruit for which Carneros Chardonnay is known. The various Cabernet Sauvignon wines here, including a budget label called Killer Cab, are powerful, rich and satisfying. The Rhone grapes are blended into a big red wine called GSM (Grenache, Syrah and Mourvedre).

SANDUZ ESTATE WINES

Here is the winery to disabuse the perception that most fruit wines are sweet. The majority of the 30 or so wines available at Sanduz—fruit wines, grape wines and blends of the two—are dry or off-dry. It reflects the palate of the owners. "I like something a little drier," says Neeta Sandhu.

OPENED 2006

12791 Blundell Road
Richmond, BC V6W 1B4

T 604.214.0444
W www.sanduzwines.com

WHEN TO VISIT
Open daily 11 am – 6 pm

Neeta and Dave Sandhu are a sophisticated and entrepreneurial couple, especially when it comes to blueberries. Among Richmond's leading growers of blueberries, they farm about 57 hectares (140 acres). The berries are sold both domestically and to a growing export market. Taking the lead from research in Japan on the health benefits of blueberries, they have developed products to make the blueberry a year-round food. They offer not only frozen and dried blueberries but powdered blueberries as food additives. The winery is a value-added extension to their business.

"There is no farming background in our families," Dave says. Born in India in 1966, he came to Canada with his parents when he was four. Nor sure what career he wanted, he studied business administration at Kwantlen College but also took courses qualifying him to work as a bailiff. Then, with a brother-in-law, he invested in a Fraser Valley blueberry farm, looking for a quick profit on real estate.

They were lucky enough to have bought the farm a month before harvest. The bushes were heavy with berries and prices were favourable. "We got the labour force in, picked the harvest, and made some good money at it," Dave recalls. And he stayed in the blueberry business.

Neeta, who was also born in India but raised in Canada, entered the wine business from an even more CONTINUED NEXT PAGE...

SANDUZ ESTATE WINES

CONTINUED

unlikely background. She has a social sciences degree from the University of Ottawa, with a major in criminology. After graduating, she joined the federal immigration department. Over a 12-year career there she worked in a variety of positions, including front-line jobs as an officer at the Vancouver International Airport. "I denied entry to people," she recalls. "I have done quasi-judicial inquiries. I've done policy and human resources. Then I said, 'I've done it all now. I want something else.'"

When the couple decided to develop a winery, they turned to Ron Taylor, the former Andrés winemaker who has reinvented himself this decade as British Columbia's busiest fruit wine consultant. Ron has rarely seen a grape or a fruit that cannot be turned into wine; and he convinced Dave and Neeta to have a large portfolio. The amazing selection includes white gooseberry, which produces a uniquely smoky wine that seems to have more in common with Sauvignon Blanc than the berry. There is wine from cranberries, raspberries, strawberries, currants, Granny Smith apples, crabapples and blackberries. And more. There is even a tasty Merlot Blueberry blended wine and a Cabernet Merlot port called Jaguar.

"I want to have something for everyone," Neeta says. Thus the winery added a selection of grape wines (Merlot, Pinot Noir, Gewürztraminer, Cabernet Sauvignon, Pinot Gris and Viognier with fruit from the Okanagan). To have vines on their property, Dave and Neeta planted just under a hectare (about two acres) of Reichensteiner vines in 2007. This white variety, created in Germany in 1939, matures to high sugar levels in cool climates. It is one of the most widely planted varieties in England, where the maritime wine-growing climate is somewhat similar to that of Richmond.

If that is not enough to choose from, visitors to the tasting room can also buy fruit syrups, jellies and honey made by bees that pollinate Dave's blueberries.

This is the place to explore the blueberry, from the dry blueberry wine to the medium dry and dessert styles, and the creative blends of blueberry and cranberry, and blueberry and Merlot. Among the grape wines, look for the Gewürztraminer and the Viognier.

NEETA AND DAVE SANDHU

TEXAS CREEK RANCH

The breathtaking aspect of this ranch, on a plateau with mountains at its back and the mighty Fraser River at its front, is as picturesque a winery location as any in British Columbia. Whether or not a winery is built depends on the results from the 1.2-hectare (three-acre) test vineyard that Eckhard Zeidler and Brad Kasselman planted here in 2008. "We are going to be growers first," Eckhard says.

Eckhard developed a hobbyist interest in vines with a tiny experimental vineyard on Salt Spring Island, on a property that proved too cool to ripen grapes adequately. Born in Vancouver in 1956, he worked in investment banking for 25 years until retiring in 1999 to run a family business in Whistler. There, he was elected to the resort's council in 2005. At subsequent municipal meetings, he met Christ'l Roshard, then the mayor of Lillooet. Christ'l and Doug Robson, her husband, had just begun a vineyard trial. Intrigued by this, Eckhard and his wife, Deanne, teamed up with Brad Kasselman to buy the 67-hectare (165-acre) Texas Creek property for grape trials of their own. Brad, who was born in Chicago in 1968 and studied Japanese in college, came to Whistler as a ski guide for Japanese visitors. He now runs the resort's major photography business.

The plum, peach and cherry trees scattered randomly around the ranch remain from a former orchard that sustained its own packing plant. These trees, along with a mature arbour of table grapes, would suggest that carefully selected varieties of wine grapes should thrive here. Eckhard and Brad planted at least 20 varieties in a four-hectare (10-acre) plot to find out what vines will prosper in a region where winters, on occasion, are cold enough to kill fruiting buds and even entire plants. They have already begun to identify winners (Auxerrois) and losers (Sauvignon Blanc). "It is like that show, Survivor," Eckhard says with a laugh. "We'll be kicking vines off the island for quite a few years."

BRAD KASSELMAN AND ECKHARD ZEIDLER

There is, in fact, a history of wine-grape trials in Lillooet. In the 1980s, Mike Galan, a Hungarian-born agriculturist, planted Baco Noir and a few other varieties in a small vineyard in the Yalacom Valley, about 25 kilometres northwest of Lillooet, on the unpaved road to Gold Bridge. He made wine as an amateur, but after his death in the early 1990s, the vineyard fell into disuse. Vines are still visible. "We passed the site last summer and the vines still [seemed] to be alive, although it is obvious that they [hadn't been] looked after in many years," Heleen Pannekoek of Fort Berens winery recounted in an email in early 2011.

PROPOSED OPENING TBC

18450 Texas Creek Road
Lillooet, BC V0K 1V0
T 250.256.0051
W www.texascreekranch.com

WHEN TO VISIT
No tasting room yet

But long before that, in the 1960s, the B.C. Electric Company planted several hybrid varieties on its Riverland Irrigated Farm here. When the farm was sold in 1972 and grape trials discontinued, Robert Roshard, the Swiss-born farm manager (and Christ'l's father) moved a selection of vines—Maréchal Foch, De Chaunac, Chancellor and Okanagan Riesling—to Roshard Acres, his home. The vines have produced reliably ever since. Christ'l and Doug Robson tend the vines (Robert died in 2008), making wine for personal consumption. "We don't need all of those grapes for our wine production," Doug admits. "And we don't contemplate ever having a winery licence."

As a councillor and then a one-term mayor of Lillooet, Christ'l—also a former editor of the newspaper—promoted grapes as an agricultural business to replace the area's closing ginseng farms and declining forestry jobs. "There is a mini-generation of people who were educated to work on the ginseng and now no longer CONTINUED NEXT PAGE...

TEXAS CREEK RANCH

had employment," she says. "I saw the wine and grape industry as something that might pick up those people." And that happened when the Fort Berens Winery planted eight hectares (20 acres) of grapes in 2009 and hired a former ginseng farm worker to manage the vineyard.

The current Lillooet grape trials began in December 2004 when Christ'l and several other Lillooet landowners secured vine cuttings in the Okanagan. With funding from the provincial government, these were propagated in a nursery. In 2005 and 2006, some 21 varieties, including all of the major vinifera grown in the Okanagan, went into test plots at three sites, including Roshard Acres, which has a stunning site on a plateau 210 metres (688 feet) above the Fraser. These plantings inspired the experimental Texas Creek Ranch planting as well as the commercial planting for Fort Berens.

The Lillooet project has enough funding to take it into 2011 and especially to continue gathering weather data from 87 electronic data collectors around Lillooet and Lytton. This is crucial information. The heat units for ripening grapes are similar to those in Osoyoos and Oliver, but there is concern that the temperature in some winters falls far enough to kill vines. On December 20, 2008, the mercury dropped to −24°C (−11°F) in Lillooet, causing bud loss and some vine loss. The Lillooet grape growers took some comfort from the fact that the winter was just as harsh in the Okanagan and the Similkameen, where crop insurance claims hit $20 million.

That winter did not discourage Eckhard and Brad at Texas Creek. The ranch has been producing premium quality hay for riding schools and racing stables. "We have a number of years of evaluation," Eckhard says of his vines. "We have to prove we can grow excellent wine grapes. If we can't do that, then we are doing other things."

WELLBROOK WINERY

It may seem a bit curious that Wellbrook, which marks its seventh anniversary in 2011 with a big summer party, calls itself a "heritage" winery—until you look around the property. This is a century-old Delta farm and looks it. The mammoth barn was once so dangerously near to collapsing that tradesmen refused to go inside. Terry Bremner, the owner of the winery, found a courageous carpenter to help him restore it. They also restored the building that serves as the winery tasting room, a century-old grain storage building now called The Old Grainery Store. It is furnished with antiques.

Terry and his mother, Caroline, bought the farm in 2001, becoming only its third owner. It was developed by Seymour Huff, a pioneering Delta farmer who operated it for 50 years before turning it over to his grandson, Gordon, who ran it for another 50 years. As an adolescent, Terry, who was born in Delta in 1959, delivered newspapers to the Huff home. Later, Terry was a member of the volunteer fire department when Gordon Huff was the chief.

OPENED 2004

4626 88th Street
Delta, BC V4K 3N3

T   604.946.1868

W   www.wellbrookwinery.com

WHEN TO VISIT
Open daily 11 am – 6 pm

TERRY BREMNER

CONTINUED NEXT PAGE...

WELLBROOK WINERY

CONTINUED

Terry was close to buying winery property elsewhere in Delta when he discovered that the Huff farm was available. "This just had so much character," he says. "It was a perfect match." Gordon provided details about the architecture and the farm's history during the two years when Terry was renovating the buildings, including the house with its wraparound veranda. The property was once called Wellbrook Farms because it had one of the few wells in the area. "I have a picture of the old windmill and the water tower," Terry says, using this history as the inspiration for the winery's name.

This is not just a winery and a working farm but also a destination where visitors can buy everything from antiques and pumpkins in season to fruit wines. Hayrides and a petting zoo are available here. The cooking school's events are usually oversubscribed. There are barn dances. Before Christmas, Terry puts up a massive display of lights. The 22-hectare (55-acre) property, just west of exit 20 on busy Highway 99, grows cranberries, blueberries and, one day, perhaps a small vineyard. Terry and a brother, Alan, also operate a 33-hectare (80-acre) blueberry farm nearby.

Terry inherited his taste for agriculture from his late father. A long-time assessor of the Corporation of Delta, Stan Bremner changed careers in the 1970s to farm. He once had a flock of 300 to 400 sheep, whose lambs were so prized that the customer list developed entirely by word of mouth. The Bremner family farm switched to blueberries in the early 1980s and again, the Bremner trademark became known for quality fruit.

The idea of a winery evolved from the fresh-juice business that Terry started in 2000, to offer ultra-premium blueberry and cranberry juices, now sold across Canada and in the United States. When The Fort Wine Co. opened in 2001, it bought Bremner blueberries and the winemaker praised the berry quality. This inspired Terry, a home fruit-winemaker for years, to contract The Fort's winemakers to make wines for Wellbrook as well. Terry took over his own winemaking in 2008 when The Fort stopped providing its services.

"You want to make a good end-product," Terry says. "In my mind, the ingredients are the most important item and that's what we do. We grow the best ingredients." With nine varieties of blueberries on his farms, Terry wonders whether there might be a place in the future for named varietals from the four now blended in the Wellbrook wines: Bluecrop, Hardyblue, Olympia and Spartan. It might be an uphill battle. "With wines, you can say specific varieties of grapes because people have been educated for 1,000 years about them," Terry says. "With blueberries, most people don't even know there is more than one variety."

MY PICKS

The winery offers seven table wines (Blueberry, Peach Apricot, White CranApple, Cranberry, BlueCran, Strawberry and Rhubarb) matched with food pairings emerging from the cooking school. Peach Apricot, for example, is recommended with spicy curries. The six dessert wines include a robust port-style Blackberry wine.

WESTHAM ISLAND ESTATE WINERY

Westham Island is another of the many wineries touched by John Harper. Berry grower Andy Bissett, who was preparing plans for the winery when he died suddenly in 2002, had concluded from Harper's grape-growing experiments in Cloverdale that wine-quality fruit and grapes could be grown on fertile Westham Island. Andy's winery licence application was stalled in Delta's bureaucracy when he died. His feisty widow, Lorraine, broke a zoning logjam by telephoning the mayor directly and, helped by daughter Tamara, got the winery open a year later. Andy is remembered by the oil painting in the winery's antique-rich tasting room, showing an amiable figure in hunting gear, surrounded by his bird-hunting friends.

The rich, 14-hectare (35-acre) Westham Island farm, owned by the Bissett family for more than a quarter-century, grows a profusion of berries, along with some rows of Concord, Maréchal Foch and Madeleine Sylvaner grapes. The cultured blackberries are menu items on cruise ships. The farm's jams, syrups and produce, which are sold at its fruit stand during the season, have a strong following.

Westham Island revived the winemaking career of Ron Taylor, a legendary British Columbia winemaker. Born in Vancouver in 1942, he went to work in 1970 at the Andrés winery in Port Moody after graduating in microbiology from the University of British Columbia. In his 22 years there, the avuncular Ron mentored many younger winemakers in his laboratory. He left Andrés to work with a bottled-water company but returned to winemaking when he consulted briefly for Columbia Valley Classics, a fruit winery that opened in 1998 at Cultus Lake. Andy met Ron there and quickly engaged him. Until then, Ron had not made fruit wines. Since then he has helped more than half a dozen fruit wineries get started.

While he tailors the wines to each winery's customers, Ron has developed a general style, with many of his fruit wines being off-dry and even sweet. "I think it's required," Ron explains. Ron makes excellent, dry fruit wines both for Westham Island and for his other clients. "But historically, if you look at fruit wines, people made them for social wines. Sweeter wines can go very well with spicy foods."

One of the winemakers famously involved in the creation of Andrés Baby Duck, Ron revisited the idea at Westham with a summertime rosé from the Concord and Maréchal Foch grapes. "It is called Just Ducky," he chuckles. It is one of the most popular wines in the tasting room. The profusion of other produce grown here gives him plenty of options to be creative. Ron makes wines from red, black and white currants, blueberries, raspberries, peaches, rhubarb, tayberries, blackberries, cranberries and even pumpkins. His personal favourite is a luscious strawberry dessert wine that he calls a milkshake for adults.

The winery's location on Westham Island, the home of the Reifel Migratory Bird Sanctuary, guarantees it many

OPENED 2003

2170 Westham Island Road
Delta, BC V4K 3N2

T 604.940.9755

W www.westhamisland
winery.com

WHEN TO VISIT
Open 11 am – 6 pm daily
in summer; check website or
call for seasonal hours

LORRAINE BISSETT

CONTINUED NEXT PAGE...

WESTHAM ISLAND ESTATE WINERY

CONTINUED

visitors, since the bird sanctuary might get 80,000 visitors each year. This is the year-round traffic that wineries need. Birdwatchers come from afar in November to see the thousands of snow geese that return to the island annually. Never missing an opportunity, the winery produces a gooseberry wine called SnoGoos.

Flat and fertile, Westham Island, 648 hectares (1,600 acres) in size, is in the mouth of the south arm of the Fraser River and has been farmed at least since 1870. In the 1920s, George C. Reifel, a successful distiller, bought land on the island for, according to local legend, shipping spirits to the United States during Prohibition. Later he developed a significant farm that, during World War II, produced sugar beets. Ultimately, his family leased, sold and donated the parcels that comprise the bird sanctuary today. Only about five percent of the island is cultivated now, growing berries, fruits and vegetables.

MY PICKS

There are a lot of toothsome wines here: Strawberry, Raspberry, Tayberry, Peach, Black Currant, Framboise, Westham White Table Wine and Just Ducky.

WINE-SPEAK:
A GLOSSARY

ACIDITY
The natural tartness in grapes and other fruit that contributes to vibrant flavours.

APPELLATION
The geographical definition of a wine region. British Columbia's current appellations are the Okanagan Valley, the Similkameen Valley, the Fraser Valley, Vancouver Island and the Gulf Islands.

BIODYNAMIC VITICULTURE
An extreme form of organic grape growing. Growers not only avoid artificial fertilizers, pesticides and herbicides, they make their own compost and cultivate beneficial bacteria for the soil, culturing it in such media as stags' bladders. It sounds weird but some of the best French wineries do it.

BOTRYTIS
A fungus that attacks grape skins. In favourable conditions (misty mornings, dry afternoons) it dehydrates grapes, allowing the production of intense dessert wines. In unfavourable conditions (too much rain) it rots the grapes. Because the climate is generally dry in the Okanagan and Similkameen valleys, botrytis is rare, and botrytis-affected wines are rarer still.

BRIX
A measure of sugar in grapes: one degree Brix equals 18 grams of sugar per litre. Mature grapes

are typically 21 to 25 Brix, which converts to 11 to 13 percent alcohol after fermentation.

CELLARED IN CANADA

This is a phrase that commercial wineries put on the label of wines made with, or blended with, imported wine. These are sometimes taken to be authentic Canadian wines because, until recently, they have been sold in the same area of liquor stores as wines, such as VQA wines, made entirely from Canadian grapes. Labels and marketing practices are now changing to create a more obvious distinction between wines made in Canada and wines bottled here with imported wine.

CIDERY

An establishment that makes apple cider.

CLONE

The mutation of a species. Growers select and propagate grape clones chosen for such desirable qualities as early ripening, vivid flavour and deep colour. Several clones of the same variety are often planted in the same vineyard. Because the flavour and texture of the wine from each clone will be a little different, wines blended from several clones are likely to be more complex.

COLD SOAK

A procedure that happens before fermentation, in which the grapes are crushed and the resulting stew of skins and juice is cooled and left for several days before fermentation begins. The object is to extract colour and flavour. *See also* Maceration.

COMMERCIAL WINERY

A BC winery that has a commercial licence and is therefore permitted to bottle and sell wine made with imported wine or grapes.

CORKED WINE

A wine that is chemically contaminated with TCA (2,4, 6-trichloroanisole). TCA contamination is usually caused by faulty corks but can also come from barrels, other cooperage or even, apparently, from wood within a cellar cleaned with chlorine solutions. Such wines smell and taste musty, a bit like an old earth cellar. While cork producers are coming to grips with the problem, some wineries now use either synthetic corks or screw-cap closures.

ESTATE WINERY
A winery with vineyards of its own. A 1978 regulation, now obsolete, required estate wineries to have at least eight hectares (20 acres) of vines. Under current regulations, these wineries are licensed as land-based wineries. They use only BC grapes or fruit. Many wineries still call themselves estate wineries, an indication that they are based on vineyards of their own.

FARM GATE WINERY
Licence created in 1989, and now obsolete, for wineries with vineyards too small to qualify as estate wineries. These are now included with the land-based wineries.

FERMENTATION
The natural process in which yeast converts sugar to alcohol.

FLINTY
A generally positive descriptor for the crisp, mineral edge noted in some unoaked white wines, such as a bone-dry Sauvignon Blanc.

FRUIT WINE
A wine made from fruit other than grapes.

GRASSY
A descriptor for the zesty, clean, vegetative aromas of grapefruit or gooseberry in certain white wines, notably Sauvignon Blanc and Sémillon. Although such aromas are okay in those varieties, they are not acceptable in red wines, being the result of slightly under-ripe grapes.

HERBACEOUS
A snooty word for "grassy."

HYBRID
Grape varieties typically developed by crossing European varieties with native North American varieties. The plant breeder's objectives include developing varieties that ripen early or resist disease or are winter-hardy.

LABRUSCA
A family of grapes native to North America and not suitable for table wines. The best-known labrusca variety is Concord.

LAND-BASED WINERIES
The new legal jargon for estate

and farm gate wineries. Generally it means they grow some of the fruit needed for their wines.

MACERATION

The process of leaving the juice or wine sitting on crushed grape skins, typically red grapes, for days at a time to draw colour and flavour from the skins into the wine.

MADERIZE

When wines take up oxygen while they age, they gradually acquire flavours resembling Madeira, a deliberately aged Spanish wine.

MERITAGE

A word (rhymes with *heritage*) created in California to identify blends made with Bordeaux grape varieties. White Meritage is a blend of Sauvignon Blanc and Sémillon; red Meritage is a blend of Merlot, Cabernet Sauvignon, Cabernet Franc and sometimes Malbec, Petit Verdot and Carmenère. Wineries using the Meritage label subscribe to quality standards of the Meritage Association.

MICRO-OXYGENATION

A fairly recent winemaking technology in which small quantities of air are bubbled deliberately through vats of fermenting red wine. The main benefits include healthier fermentations (which need oxygen) and wines that are softer and ready to drink earlier.

MUST

Unfermented grape pulp or juice. There is no relationship between this term and the word "musty," which describes mouldy aromas.

OLD VINES

Various wineries release wines labelled as "old vines." There is no strict rule defining how old vines must be for such wine. As a rule, the vines should be at least 25 years old. A new vineyard only produces its first full crop in its third year. The majority of vineyards in British Columbia are no more than 10 to 15 years old. Fruit from old vines is prized because it can yield wines of intense flavour and great character.

ORGANIC

A technique for growing grapes (and other plants) or making wine without using chemicals such as pesticides, herbicides or commercial fertilizers. To maintain their organic certification, vineyards and wineries must be regularly audited by industry associations.

OXIDIZED

Wines that have been exposed to too much air for too long and have become flat and stale; the colour becomes dull, turning to a tired gold with white wines. It is rare to come across such wines these days, but if you do, it means the bottle on the tasting bar has been open for several days or, even worse, the winemaking techniques are dodgy.

PUMP-OVER

During red wine fermentation, the skins are buoyed by the escaping carbon dioxide and float to the top of the wine vats. This is called the cap. Several times each day, wine is pumped over the cap. The main objective of submerging the skins periodically is to make sure colour and flavour are extracted. It also prevents bacteria from growing in the cap.

SCREW CAPS

Replacing corks in wine bottles with screw caps still upsets the traditionalists, who equate caps with plonk. If that is what you think, get over it. There are few better closures for keeping white wines crisp, fresh and clean-tasting. There is still some debate as to whether screw caps are also best for red wines, but the evidence is encouraging.

SPITTING

Wineries are probably the only place where spitting is acceptable. (Okay, maybe in baseball dugouts as well.) In the interest of remaining sober, both winery staff and guests who taste wines are not obliged to swallow them. Winery tasting bars provide spittoons. In the winery itself, it is okay to spit into the drainage grates. Off-target spitters should practise before touring.

STELVIN

The trademarked name for a French design of screw cap closures for wine bottles.

TANNIN

A substance in the skin and seeds of grapes that is essential in providing backbone to red wines. When there is excessive tannin, wines are hard on the palate and have a bitter aftertaste, not unlike overly strong tea. Harsh tannins will soften during several years of bottle aging or when young reds are decanted before serving.

TERROIR

The French term that encompasses the entire environment, including the soil, climate and exposure, that defines the particular character of each vineyard.

TOASTY

A descriptor for a slightly burnt note in the aroma and sometimes the flavour of a wine that has been aged in a barrel whose interior was deliberately charred. This can be considered positive in Chardonnay and Pinot Noir because, like a pinch of salt, it adds an extra note of interest.

VARIETAL

A wine for which the constituent grape variety is named on the label (such as Chardonnay or Merlot). Such wines must contain a minimum of 85 percent of the named variety.

VINIFERA

The species of classic wine grapes that have spread from the vineyards of Europe to wherever fine wine is made.

VQA (VINTNERS QUALITY ALLIANCE)

All BC wines bearing the VQA seal must be made from BC grapes. The wines are all screened by a professional tasting panel. Wines found faulty cannot be sold as VQA wines. A number of BC wineries—including very competent producers—have chosen, for various reasons, not to submit wines for the VQA seal.

WINERY LISTINGS

Vancouver Island South

Southern Gulf Islands

Vancouver Island North

Fraser Valley

Vancouver